Selling Services

Patrick Forsyth

- Fast-track route to effective service selling within a dynamic and globally competitive marketplace

- Covers the special approaches that make selling any kind of service both acceptable to clients and an effective part of the overall marketing mix. Also looks at practical ways of dealing with high customer expectations

- Case studies drawn from a wide number of service businesses including airlines, hotels, and financial and professional services

- Includes a comprehensive resources guide, key concepts and thinkers, a 10-step action plan, and a section of FAQs

>> EXPRESS EXEC.COM <<
essential management thinking at your fingertips

SALES

12.06

First Published 2003 by
Capstone Publishing Limited (a Wiley company)
8 Newtec Place
Magdalen Road
Oxford OX4 1RE
United Kingdom
http://www.capstoneideas.com

CIP catalogue records for this book are available from the British Library and the US Library of Congress

ISBN 1-84112-459-1

Printed and bound in Great Britain by CPI Antony Rowe, Eastbourne

Substantial discounts on bulk quantities of Capstone Books are available to corporations, professional associations and other organizations. For details telephone Capstone Publishing on (+44-1865-798623), fax (+44-1865-240941) or email (info@wiley-capstone.co.uk).

Contents

Introduction to ExpressExec

ExpressExec is a completely up-to-date resource of current business practice, accessible in a number of ways – anytime, anyplace, anywhere. ExpressExec combines best practice cases, key ideas, action points, glossaries, further reading, and resources.

Each module contains 10 individual titles that cover all the key aspects of global business practice. Written by leading experts in their field, the knowledge imparted provides executives with the tools and skills to increase their personal and business effectiveness, benefiting both employee and employer.

ExpressExec is available in a number of formats:

» **Print** – 120 titles available through retailers or printed on demand using any combination of the 1200 chapters available.
» **E-Books** – e-books can be individually downloaded from ExpressExec.com or online retailers onto PCs, handheld computers, and e-readers.
» **Online** – http://www.expressexec.wiley.com/ provides fully searchable access to the complete ExpressExec resource via the Internet – a cost-effective online tool to increase business expertise across a whole organization.

» **ExpressExec Performance Support Solution (EEPSS)** – a software solution that integrates ExpressExec content with interactive tools to provide organizations with a complete internal management development solution.

» **ExpressExec Rights and Syndication** – ExpressExec content can be licensed for translation or display within intranets or on Internet sites.

To find out more visit www.ExpressExec.com or contact elound@wiley-capstone.co.uk.

Introduction to Selling Services

Selling is a vital strategic and tactical part of the marketing mix, briefly described as:

» an essential process;
» an essentially manageable process.

"Everyone lives by selling something"

Robert Louis Stevenson

Though part of the marketing mix, selling is sometimes overshadowed by more complex or fashionable techniques and can thus be regarded as a poor relation of marketing.

It is in no way any such thing.

Selling is a vital strategic and tactical part of the marketing mix, and in many industries it is the final link in the marketing chain between an organization and its customers. In such cases, however well implemented other aspects of the marketing mix may be, they achieve nothing if the quality of execution of personal selling is not of a high order. It is selling that converts the interest generated by other promotional communications into actual business.

Perhaps nowhere is selling more likely to be underestimated than when the "product" is a service. Sometimes it is felt that a service speaks for itself, and that no selling is really necessary. Sometimes, perhaps especially in small businesses, the people involved are experts in the delivery of the service; selling is not their stock-in-trade, indeed sometimes too overt a sales role is seen as actually diluting the image the service is at pains to present.

AN ESSENTIAL PROCESS

Yet in every case sales is essential. Services may vary; they include broad categories such as travel (hotels and airlines, for example), business services (from market research to computer maintenance), retail services (from dry cleaning to interior design), and many more. They also include the important sector of professional services: those selling professional and technical services on some sort of fee basis and including accountants, lawyers, surveyors, architects, and many kinds of consultant. This sector in turn overlaps into financial services, which again encompasses a wide range of different things, from banking to insurance and more.

Selling is a social skill. It is a communications skill. And, as anyone who has been involved in a breakdown of communications knows, communicating clearly – *but you didn't say that!* – is not guaranteed to be easy. In selling the communication must:

» be clear;
» persuade;
» differentiate.

All three are important and thus selling is something that must be done right; and with some precision.

NOT ROCKET SCIENCE

Selling involves a variety of approaches and techniques. It is not rocket science, nor is it unmanageably intellectually taxing. But it is complex. There is a great deal going on in the interaction and a lot to bear in mind for those trying to do it well. The complexity comes from the need to deploy skills appropriately, keep all the balls in the air, and maximize the chances of success throughout the process.

Two other things are vital:

» *Selling is a bespoke activity*: there is no – repeat no – one right way to sell services, or anything else for that matter. It is *not* a question of scripting the approach or going about things by rote. Effective selling is that deployed client by client, day by day, meeting by meeting. It is what works for a particular circumstance today. Tomorrow, certainly next week or next year, something a little different will be necessary.
» *Selling is a fragile process:* success is, to a large extent, in the details. One seemingly small thing omitted or handled inappropriately can result in rejection. Something done especially well (matching *this* client especially well) can make a disproportionately positive difference. You need to keep on your toes and be quick on your feet.

I can probably type as well now as I ever will (not perfectly, but fast enough for what I do). Provided I continue to type regularly my skills will be maintained, and unless the "querty" keyboard is replaced no further learning will be necessary. Selling is not like that. We can all spend a lifetime learning to sell. It is a dynamic skill and must be applied appropriately "on the day." Even then success is not guaranteed; no one wins them all – the best technique maximizes strike rate and that is as much as can be hoped for.

Selling was never easy. Today, in competitive and dynamic markets it can be damned difficult. Selling intangible services presents special problems and demands specific approaches. It is these that this book examines. There is no magic formula that guarantees sales success (though I must have been asked what *the* secret is on every sales training course I have ever conducted). There are, however, certainly some things – of which more anon – which have a particularly strong impact, but one thing is a necessary foundation: that is, the view taken of the process by whoever is doing the selling. To put that in context, let me say that – based on my observation and experience – the most successful people in selling are those who take the trouble to understand how the process works. They work at deploying the techniques in the best possible way in light of that understanding.

Here we review a variety of aspects of the specific task of selling services successfully. This review cannot guarantee success, but it could help put you in a position where you can succeed.

Note: the message that follows is addressed primarily to the person doing the selling, whomever that may be. This includes everyone from full-time, dedicated field sales people to those who must sell as part of other, perhaps senior, jobs, including the consultant and the general manager. Managers interested in the sales performance of others, including members of a sales team, may also find the *ExpressExec* volume *Sales Management* useful (as the author of that too, I am no doubt prejudiced, but if a book on selling cannot contain a justified plug, what can?). A final introductory point: terminology varies, but most service providers sell to "clients" rather than "customers," and the first word thus appears most here.

What is Selling Services?

Services need promoting just like anything else, and this chapter kicks off with a couple of examples before covering the following topics:

» people are the product;
» the nature of the process;
» the structure of the task.

"I've never bought anything from salespeople who didn't know their product and yet I have bought things I didn't know I needed from people who did"
Mark McCormack, American sports agent and
author of the book McCormack on Selling

There is a school of thought that suggests that if you can sell one thing you can sell anything. Usually this is simply untrue. Services are different. Yet they are not specially protected from competitiveness and the dynamism of the marketplace. Like any other business they prosper only by attracting sufficient clients prepared to pay sufficient money at the right time. If the service is good, surely people will seek it out and profitable business will result?

This does not, in fact, just happen. Services need promoting just like anything else, and selling – personal selling – is an important part of the promotional mix. Service selling poses particular challenges, primarily for one main reason – services are intangible.

An insurance policy, a research survey, a training course, some graphic design – how does anyone know, in advance, and having not used a particular supplier previously, that they are making the right choice in selecting one rather than another?

They cannot know.

There are literally *no* guarantees. Service suppliers usually expect to get agreement, sign people up (even get them paying something up front) – and only then for their clients to find out whether their work is any good or not. At least that is how it seems to the clients. They like the greater certainty that comes with buying a product. You can test drive the car. You can try on a suit, you can feel the material, match it to a tie, and compare it with those in the shop next door. If purchase then follows it is with a feeling that some considerable likelihood exists of the product being what the customer wants.

Selling a service has to get over this: it has to instil confidence in a way that makes up for the lack of certainty. A graphic designer may show brochures that he or she has designed in the past, but however good they are it does not automatically imply that the next clients will be equally happy with what is done for them. Very often a crucial part of selling is to stimulate the prospect's imagination, making something intangible seem real, and going further – making people imagine actually using and benefiting from the service. Failure to accept the need for this can quickly dilute sales effectiveness (see the example below, reproduced from my *ExpressExec* title *Sales Management*).

EXAMPLE

Some of my work is in the hotel industry. In one recent project, talking with a sales team about the sale of meeting and conference facilities (a major area of business for many properties), I touched on the use of photographs as a simple kind of sales aid. After all, if a prospect seeking a venue for a training course, a banquet, or a wedding is shown into an empty room, as is often the way, then it is asking a good deal of them. They must imagine it laid out in just the way that will make their unique function a success. Realistically it is not a degree of imagination to be assumed.

All that was available was brochures produced a few years before, and just before the hotel first opened. These – presumably because the hotel was not yet operating at the time they were originated – showed only empty rooms; hardly a spur to the customers' imagination (and not so uncommon in the industry). Yet the sales director rejected a suggestion that some money should be spent creating a small portfolio of new shots – with immediate concern for the budget.

So, it would have cost some money, though not too much. But the alternative was that many of their prospects, who are very likely to check out more than one venue, will find this particular aspect of the sale more impressive elsewhere. In a competitive business, ignoring this kind of detail is simply risking letting business go by default. This was in a five-star and well-known hotel.

Furthermore, sales approaches must combat the frame of mind brought to bear by the prospect. The uncertainty they feel may be just that, uncertainty, or feelings may run higher, reflecting circumstances on the buyer's side (see the box overleaf).

EXAMPLE

Prospects may be feeling:

» *suspicious* (as people all too often are of someone selling);
» *exposed* (if they hire you what does it mean for *them*?); or
» *embarrassed* (shouldn't they be able to do what they are asking you to do?).

In addition, they may be upset because something is overdue for attention, needs to be put right (perhaps attracting blame to them for its current state), puts pressure on them (say of time), or any of a dozen different factors. Such things are more likely and more personal than in the situation of buying tangible products and an appropriate measure of sensitivity is needed in the seller to overcome them.

Many of these will be heightened where the cost and importance of the service is high.

The point here is that many potentially negative feelings are to be expected on occasion. There are good reasons for them to exist, and sellers should not resent their existence. Correctly identifying how buyers feel and matching your approach to it, reassuring not just in a general sense, but also specifically addressing the particular fears in a prospect's mind, will add power to your selling.

PEOPLE ARE THE PRODUCT

Services are nothing without people. Potential clients tend not to meet the service deliverers first, they meet people intent on selling to them. In some cases, of course, this does mean that they meet a service provider – perhaps a technical person like a surveyor – wearing sales hat.

People must combine the two roles to some degree. In many organizations it helps if service providers have an involvement in selling (as has been said, sometimes the two things are combined), in which case they must sell well. Conversely, people selling must be aware that they are an inherent part of the service and that that is on show as they sell. I conduct many courses in hotel meeting rooms. If I check out a hotel and arrange a meeting with one of its sales people and that person is late for it, what does it say? Not simply that they are not as efficient as they might be, but that their organization may not be as efficient as I want. When I say *Let's take a break*, will the coffee be outside, hot and ready, even if I am 10 minutes early or late from the planned break time? Something as simple as a missed appointment or a phone call not returned promptly may suggest not. How easy do I find it to buy then? Enough. The point is clear: in selling a service, service and sales are inherently tied together.

THE NATURE OF THE PROCESS

The fear amongst many in service sectors, especially professional services, that too overt a style of selling, what many would call pushy, will negate the businesslike relationship they want to create between them, is a common one. It is a real one too, but only if the seller takes the wrong view of the sales process. Selling is not something you can regard as "doing to people." This makes the process seem inappropriately one way, when it should be a dialog.

The best definition I know of selling is that it is "helping people to buy." This seems simple, but characterizes the process well. Prospects want to go through a process of decision making, indeed they will do so whatever the seller may do. So, the core of what makes the basis for sales technique is twofold and both elements start on the client's side of the relationship. First, we must consider the way in which people buy. Much as anybody does when buying anything else, those buying services investigate options and weigh up the pros and cons of any given case (and often, of course, they are intentionally checking out several competing options alongside each other).

How do they do this? They go through a particular sequence of thinking. One way of looking at this, summarized by psychologists way back, is paraphrased here. They say to themselves:

» I am important and want to be respected.
» Consider my needs.
» Will your ideas help me?
» What are the facts?

» What are the snags?
» What shall I do?
» I approve/disapprove.

Each step in the process must be taken before the buyer will willingly move on to the next one. Some decisions can be taken at once, while others require a pause between each stage. The core of this process is that the buyer is weighing up the pros and cons of making a decision. Buyers want to be able to make an appropriately informed decision; they metaphorically put different points on one side of a balance or the other. Nothing is perfect, so what wins is better thought of as what has the best balance. In competitive situations a case can be won, or lost, on the basis of just one or two small points swinging the balance one way or another.

In buying services, decisions certainly follow this seven-stage process. But execution of the process can be much more complex due to the nature of the client's business; the size of the organization; the people and functions involved; their needs; and the degree of influence they have on buying decisions – and what they are buying. For example, considering with whom to commission a major consultancy study is likely to be a more complex process than deciding where to get a car serviced. Selling is best viewed from this perspective. As has been said, it is not something that you do *to* people – it is the mirror image of the buying process – something that is inherently two way.

Selling is a process of need satisfaction and research shows two facts that are extremely valuable to sellers. First, sales meetings are much more successful when the client's needs are clearly identified. Second, they are less successful when those needs are only implied. Asking is thus as important as telling.

Nothing is successfully sold unless a client willingly buys. This is encouraged by offering satisfied needs as reasons for buying, i.e., perfect holes, not precision drills; reduced administrative costs, not computer programs. To follow the buying mind's seven-step process is vital in selling any kind of service. There is a need to relate closely what is done in selling to the client's point of view; this can only be done if it is thought through carefully. Your sales approach must therefore be another key factor stated in one word: planned.

Selling a service fits well with this concept. You are in the business of playing a part in your potential clients' decision-making processes, assisting them to make decisions – the right ones – rather than pressurizing them into it. The service seller must be, in part, an advisor. Being an advisor simply does not fit with a high-pressure approach.

If the right approach is adopted and accepted, sales are more likely to be confirmed; indeed, some approaches that assist persuasiveness will come over as part of the service philosophy of the service provider (some techniques that achieve this are highlighted in Chapter 6, The State of the Art).

THE STRUCTURE OF THE TASK

The actual task facing those aiming to sell services can be described across a number of stages:

» *Prospect identification:* Some prospects identify themselves. They are recommended to you or respond to your promotion perhaps. In many businesses an active approach is necessary too. It is necessary to decide whom to see (and whom not to) and to put some priorities to prospects. This may need following up by promotional or sales action: using a variety of techniques from direct mail to cold calling.
» *Planning:* With prospects in mind, and a meeting in prospect, some preparation is necessary. The best sales people do not just ''wing it,'' they create an approach tailored to achieve their aims and matched to each particular prospect they meet.
» *Handling the sales meeting:* Selling needs approaching systematically; a meeting needs some structure and must be designed to take an amount of time acceptable to the prospect. The plan is like a route map, as important to assist when it is not possible to follow the planned route as it is when we can. The course of a meeting cannot be dictated; it must follow the input of the prospect to some degree even though you will want to keep it as much as possible on *your* track.

In thinking through the best approach, it helps to consider the logical stages of a meeting:

» *Opening:* the first moments, making a good first impression, identifying needs, and setting the scene for the way you want to describe your service.

» *Presentation:* making your case, and making it understandable, attractive, and credible to ensure it can act persuasively. How this is done, the power and precision of your description and more are vital to success.

» *Handling objections:* any sales pitch is likely to give rise to some objections (which may in any case only be clarifying questions) and this stage too must be handled smoothly.

» *Gaining a commitment ("closing"):* closing does not cause people to buy, but it is often (usually?) necessary to take the initiative and *ask* for the business, converting the interest you have generated into actual orders.

The job here is multifaceted. The overall progress of the meeting must be controlled and managed, and at the same time individual sales techniques must be deployed as appropriate and how things are done adjusted in the light of how the meeting is going.

» *Follow-up:* A simple description of a far-reaching activity. If the prospect agrees, then the contact needs maintaining. If he hesitates, persistent chasing needs to take place, and yet be made acceptable. Beyond that, those that become regular accounts need managing and strategies developing to secure, develop, and build future business.

SUMMARY

The sales job is far from routine (despite much about its image). It needs a careful, systematic, and creative approach demanding considerably more precision in the way it is done than the application of the traditional "gift of the gab." Service selling is a particular challenge because of the intangible nature of the "product." Success is therefore more dependent on the people aspects and on the detail of how things are approached and described. The key to it all is seeing things from the point of view of the client – the classic sales empathy – and using that to fine-tune approaches to ensure both persuasiveness and an approach which is acceptable to, and appeals to, the client.

The Evolution of Selling Services

Like products, services have long needed selling. This chapter describes how the concept of selling services has evolved since the Second World War, covering the following topics:

» reputation;
» progress;
» today – the true importance.

"When the more entrepreneurial Neanderthals were trading axe heads – three for the price of two, and I'll throw in a spare handle – in exchange for, say, a week's supply of mammoth pie, there was little choice. Mammoth pie might not be the gastronomic treat of the millennium, but deep pan pizza was in short supply so if you wanted axe heads – no choice"

From Marketing stripped bare *(Kogan Page)*

Like products, services have long needed selling. In times of low choice prior to the marketing revolution of the 1950s and 60s there really were situations where choice was so limited that some things needed little or no selling. Once choice began to expand (effectively in the years after the Second World War), competition increased and selling became necessary.

REPUTATION

There are plenty of signs that in the earliest days of selling customers were suspicious of sales people, indeed they seem to have had reason to be. Even the language reflects this: we refer to being swindled as "being sold a pup" or "being sold down the river" and we hear (still) some sales people talking with some contempt about customers, referring for instance to "punters."

Sadly, selling still has a less than perfect reputation today. We talk of "high pressure" selling, "pushy" sales people, and if their daughter comes home and says her latest boyfriend sells double glazing then amongst the reactions of many parents is to lock up the family silver. While this sort of attitude is directed primarily towards products such as double glazing, home improvements of various kinds, and timeshare, its existence hardly helps anyone in more respectable areas, including services. Indeed there are developments that act to perpetuate it, such as the recent news coverage of the sale of various investment and pension products. In addition, there is the ongoing popularity of the various "consumer" television programs, some of which focus on fringe areas (the driving instructor from hell) but still lend support to the overall feeling.

This lingering lack of recognition of the true worth of the sales role does selling and sales people no good:

» with customers or clients, some at least of whom are as a result disposed to treat everything any salesperson says as a barefaced lie, or at least with some suspicion;

» internally within organizations, where sales people are still sometimes regarded as lower in status than they deserve. Some people inside an organization, largely through ignorance perhaps, think selling is an easy job – *swanning about in a car all day chatting to people*. Thus something of a "them and us" situation can develop within groups, some of which may adversely affect customer service as people fail to work well together.

If you are in a sales role – make no mistake – you do something important. If selling is among your portfolio of tasks, do not sideline it or feel it is somehow of less status than your other tasks. It is a necessary task and it demands skill; by no means everyone can sell successfully (as this book no doubt makes clear).

PROGRESS

In the years up to the 1960s, selling was just, well, selling, at worst viewed as an unfortunate necessity rather than as a marketing tool as important as any other.

The increasing way in which management came to be regarded as needing to be professional in the years beyond affected selling also. Business was becoming more competitive. In the United Kingdom the Industrial Training Boards were using financial incentives to persuade organizations to increase training (and this involved both sales and sales management training along with many other management techniques). And the gurus were beginning to carve out a place in the business scene with sales as one area of focus (Heinz Goldman's regular sell-out seminars on sales technique led the way).

As a different view of selling emerged, so did recognition that selling was not one generic mish-mash. It mattered what was being sold and it was recognized that different fields needed different approaches.

In the early 1970s, sales training became ever more usual and ever more practical. Selling, in the sense of "doing things to people," became less the way and most training became based on the essential psychology of the selling/buying process. The most high-profile early exponent of this approach was probably the Huthwaite Group whose research-based courses and books featured what they called the SPIN approach to selling; one that formalized the psychological approach more than most.

Cost and customers

Two other factors became important in the changes towards greater and greater professionalism: the first was cost. As it became more and more expensive to employ good sales people, and the total costs include recruitment and selection, training, management and support, the expenses incurred in travel and operation as well as salaries and any incentives, so the job they did changed. The trend over many years now has been for organizations to employ fewer but more professional people.

Customers too have become more demanding and are better at, and in some cases better trained for, the buying role. Sales people have to relate to them and do so as far as possible as equals. Another trend here is the power increasingly wielded by the major buyers – big customers or clients are not just larger than others, they are different from others (certainly the impact of losing one is!) – and this needs more sophisticated handling. Major sales need more planning and the quality of the person doing the selling is paramount.

Those selling services may, in some instances, have lagged these trends somewhat, but today they inhabit a specialist area and must be as competent and professional as those selling any other kind of product.

One sector of services is worth a particular word, as its development has followed a concentrated and accelerated path over the past 15 years or so (see box: Professional services).

PROFESSIONAL SERVICES

The historical development of these areas (from accountancy to surveying) is worth a separate word. Those involved in these areas view themselves as professionals with a capital P, as indeed they well might – the training involved to become, say, a lawyer is not insubstantial. But in the past this led to their standing apart from the rough world of competition and what, as *The Forsyte Saga* reminded us again recently, used to be called "trade." Their work came by recommendation and the professional bodies governing these businesses were alike in actually forbidding such devices as marketing (and particularly advertising and selling).

The relaxation of these "ethical" restrictions was led by the accountants in the 1980s. It produced a sea change in the way these businesses work. Suddenly not only was marketing activity possible, it rapidly became necessary and doing it well became as important as doing the technical work well. There was an almost frantic search for knowledge and expertise (I remember conducting marketing appreciation courses early on in this period at the Institute of Chartered Accountants. It was characteristic of the times that there were always some people who walked out of these sessions saying something like – *if this is what marketing is, I want nothing to do with it.* Sorry, I digress.)

Gradually, marketing practices have been adopted and, to large measure, made to work in all the professions. After all, services may be different from products, and professional services more different still, but they are in no way protected from competition. They need the right volume of fee-earning work, at the right time and at the right price, and, these days, there must be an active and systematic approach to achieving just that. Selling caused particular problems in adoption. It makes the point about its reputation, and there are plenty still in such firms who would not dream of actually using the word "sales," however much they know that business must be found and that a major amount of what does that is achieved through personal communication. The euphemisms still abound, but client or business development or whatever still encompasses sales.

That said, the professional of today is often excellent at selling. Selling has gradually become not only part of the routine, and one of the necessary skills, but part of the personal satisfaction too. Everyone likes it when a deal is agreed; even professionals now find satisfaction in signing up a new client and being able to look at the chain of events that preceded it and say – *I made that happen.*

TODAY – THE TRUE IMPORTANCE

The role of selling in the service sector is now both clear and important. Key are the following:

» Selling is not only a key part of the marketing mix, it is often the final link in a chain of events that occur between the organization and its clients; literally, without personal selling the marketing process could not complete its job of bringing in the business
» Unlike other marketing techniques, selling is a personal and often one-to-one process. In selling services, people must inform, persuade, and differentiate; they must also often offer, and make credible, advice and act themselves as an example of the quality of service to come
» Selling fits, indeed must be made to fit, the way in which people buy services. The method and the manner must act to give people what they want, to fulfill expectations and assist the buying decision-making process that will take place and that buyers *want* to take place
» Selling creates and must maintain and develop the business relationship that is an inherent part of buying services, and particularly do so regularly
» Buyers must see the process of selling of services, in terms of how it is carried out, as an efficient and useful process. They do not want something done *to them*; they want support and assistance in making the right decision.

Above all, the intangible nature of services means that the power of description, the way in which an individual personifies the service and the organization that provides it and the precision with which the task is approached must all be of a high order.

Selling a service is not the easiest kind of selling, but it is one where the effect of a sound and well-considered approach on the outcome is very direct.

Finally

A small, but significant point: the terminology has changed, because the people have changed. Everyone selling used to be called a salesman. This reflected less politically correct times, but also the fact that the vast majority of people in such jobs were men. Gradually this has changed. Many women are now in selling, and the proportion involved in selling services is higher than in many areas. The words "sales person" now encompass many different kinds of job, including those selling on the telephone or in retail situations. The salesman is long gone, and those who do full-time external sales jobs are now better called field sales people. In addition, a host of other titles exist, from sales executive to senior account management director (some of these reflect the range of more sophisticated jobs that must now be done, others are frankly euphemisms designed only to make jobs sound more sophisticated).

The sales job will doubtless continue to evolve, with exactly what it encompasses developing over time. It will also remain an important, maybe vital, part of the overall marketing process.

The E-Dimension

There is no doubt that information technology has changed the arena in which business operates forever. The implications are reviewed in turn:

- » client attitudes;
- » customers' systems;
- » suppliers' implications;
- » multiple impacts on the sales process;
- » best practice.

"Technology is like a bus. If it goes in the direction you want to go, take it"

Renzo Piano

There is no doubt that information technology has changed the arena in which business operates forever. The process continues and, while it is fruitless to predict (who was it who said that prediction is easy, it's getting it right that's hard?), it is necessary to cope with what is current and to anticipate, at least to a certain extent, what may come next.

The first thing to be acknowledged is that the IT revolution has created many new things to be sold; some of these are services. There are companies offering to design software, to service computers, and to install and maintain high-tech systems of all sorts. It is difficult to sell such services without familiarity with the technology, indeed in many cases without considerable expertise in it. Describing something both intangible and technical demands precise communications skills, especially if selling is, perhaps necessarily, addressed to non-technical people on the client side.

On the other hand, such services need to reflect the same approaches as any other service and the lessons reviewed elsewhere all apply here, though the application of them may need to reflect the special nature of any one situation.

The impact of this ongoing revolution also affects the sale of any service, not just those bound up with the technology. The implications fall predominately into a small number of categories. These are reviewed in turn.

CLIENT ATTITUDES

Clients live in the wired world. They expect certain things to have an e-dimension. They may see this as useful or they may be wary of it, or actively annoyed by it. Douglas Adams (he of *Hitchhikers' Guide to the Galaxy* fame) says in his last book, published posthumously after his sad and early death, "Anything invented after you're thirty-five is against the natural order of things." Some clients feel this way.

The different attitudes that exist towards the e-revolution, and its conveniences and hazards, must be borne in mind. As with so much else, individual approaches are necessary and they must be well-judged.

For example, even something as simple as suggesting that someone checks something on your Website may prompt very different reactions. One person may accept it as the best way forward, another may see it as unhelpful, time wasting, and wonder why you are not offering a brochure or fact sheet.

CUSTOMERS' SYSTEMS

On the other hand, you should respect and utilize client systems and make doing so when requested entirely natural. Again this affects simple things as well as more complicated ones. If someone asks for something to be e-mailed (planning perhaps to copy it at a touch of a button to others), then e-mail it. If it is a proposal it may still be worth sending a smart paper copy as well to maximize the way in which presentation can assist your pitch. Certainly such things are worth a thought, and you must not fall into an "automatic pilot" reflex of doing things one particular way – especially not judging it only by what is easiest for you.

SUPPLIERS' IMPLICATIONS

Here the task is twofold: first, responding to clients needs and fitting in with the technological developments at their end of things, second, seeking opportunities to improve efficiency, service, and sales effectiveness by the action you take.

Some, perhaps much, of the initiative here lies with management, primarily sales and marketing management. Such is beyond our brief here. But there are things that can be done at sales level too, whatever the nature and position of the person doing the selling. Ideas – good ideas – do not care who has them. The nature of the sales job has a repetitive element to it. The good thing about that is that it allows accelerated practice: if the people selling the service do not have ideas about improving sales methodology, then who does? Especially for those with an interest in technology, there is an opportunity to act as a catalyst. Many times I have seen ideas generated by individual sales people adopted throughout an organization and then act to improve sales practice. This is a good general principle, but especially so of a fast-changing area like technology (and as one sales person said to me – *my manager doesn't know one end of a computer from another*).

MULTIPLE IMPACTS ON THE SALES PROCESS

All sorts of things of a technological nature are involved in the sales process; many are useful and enhance the process, but all need care. Comment is made on a list of such things, starting with a simple one:

» *Mobile telephones:* these are already ubiquitous and their use can certainly boost customer service and speed things up; but they should *never* ring and interrupt a client meeting. They seem headed to duplicate some of what computers do, though how well they will do so remains to be seen. Swift contact with people can enhance service, and all aspects of service are doubly important in selling service "products."

» *Mobile computers:* these, in the form of everything from high capacity laptops to simpler handheld devices (e.g. Palm or Psion machines), can go into the customer meeting with you. They allow a variety of things to be done quickly and easily:
  » checking availability and placing an order for clients as you sit in their own office during a visit;
  » updating records or issuing instructions to the sales office (perhaps from the car after a meeting); and
  » forming part of a presentation to a customer (using PowerPoint charts to explain complex figures perhaps).

The net impact here should be good: saving time, adding immediacy and allowing informed decisions to be made on the spot.

» *Information update:* a variety of information can be put over by learning packages (e.g. programmed learning devices on CD-ROM). This may be useful for "product" knowledge updating and providing a ready source of reference and checking too. You may also find training beamed to you this way; such rarely provides a complete answer, but always adopting a positive attitude to it is sensible, whatever else may be needed to complete the picture and link to the actual job.

» *Communications:* methods have changed (when did you last get a telex or even a fax?) and e-mail has replaced many more complex messages. It takes time to get something written, printed out, and posted, so the convenience – especially to someone on the move – is obvious. But it is not right for everything. An e-mail may fail to impress a client by being too informal, or it may prove so brief that it fails to be clear. And it can be wiped out at the touch of a button (so may not produce any potentially lasting memory-jogger with a client), and it does not impress graphically in the way a company letterhead should. Horses for courses – a variety of communication methods must still be used, and if you always go for the easy option it may dilute the overall and cumulative impression you should be working to build.

» *Research and information:* information is power, it is said. Going to a meeting under-informed and showing that no trouble has been taken to find out about a new potential client can quickly do damage. A while ago, a few minutes on the telephone, with reference books, or spent getting hold of a company's annual report was worthwhile. Now the ability to access the Website of so many different organizations speeds and simplifies the whole process – though more than just this may be necessary, and you do have actually to *note* information obtained and think about how it can help you sell. Websites are similarly a good way to gather competitive intelligence.

» *CRM (customer relationship management) systems:* here there is considerable sophistication with many different software systems available to record, monitor, and prompt action with major clients. The data available here is invaluable, but the mistake should not be made of thinking that the system will actually do it all. Contact is personal and whatever prompt is given it must be interpreted sensibly and appropriate action then taken. As with many a system, a specific element of danger here is a lack of flexibility, with the system being followed slavishly and action directed at individual customers not being sufficiently well tailored. You probably have to use what you are instructed to use, but remember that only feedback about it will enable management to refine and improve it. Speak out if necessary.

» *Presentations:* in selling many services the sales process involves the regular use of formal presentations (another important personal skill), and in these and in many meetings visual aids are often very professional looking; anything *ad hoc* can look slapdash. Such aids are important in assisting and augmenting clients' imagination; they must *support* what is said, however, and not take over the process. If well used they add an important additional dimension to the sales process, if not they can lull you into ceasing to think sufficiently clearly; and you find you are going through presentations on automatic pilot led by the charts or whatever you are using.

» *Your organization's Website:* sales people have always had to link precisely with other media, building on the image of the organization and taking the client further in terms of both information and image. Those organizations that have Websites now have an additional element to assist in informing clients. This may mean that by the time they sit down to talk with you they are better informed than in the past (and this includes the information they have about competition, competitive prices, etc.). A good Website can thus make the job easier for sales people, but even small deficiencies can cause problems (e.g. if it is difficult to navigate or manifestly not kept up to date). You may be specifically briefed to collect and record information that will keep your site up-to-date.

» There are specific ways also that client visits to Websites can be used to enhance the sales process:

  » *Research:* information can be gathered by prompting clients or enquirers to complete information (without making it manda-tory or too onerous so to do). A well-designed Website can thus provide ongoing, up-to-date information about clients – their feel-ings, requirements, and more. If this sort of information is available in your organization, find it and use it.

  » *Telephone link:* software (or support) is available now to link client Website visits to direct contact. A client visiting a Website and wanting to take things further can click on a box and prompt telephone contact. Systems can ensure this happens promptly – or even guarantee that it happens so quickly that a call is received while the client is online: they can look at information on-screen while talking to a sales person. You may be involved in this sort of thing; you may have to pick up the thread after such conversations and need to have the right information passed to you to allow you to create good continuity.

The possibilities here are broad and varied. Any technology used alongside sales contact must be well thought out. It must be client oriented and enhance service and satisfaction rather than just improving the basis for selling and the likelihood of success (though it should do this too!). There are other implications here also. These include: selling overseas (where immediacy and quality of contact can be improved); and demonstration of commitment (someone may be impressed by the contact provided by a Website). Further technological developments will extend such possibilities further; who knows what lies ahead?

BEST PRACTICE

Now, the following two examples from real life illustrate the cross-over between technology and the more personal aspects of selling a service. First, something that did not work:

» *Bad:* Recently I was visited by a salesman in financial services (whose organization had better remain nameless). He arrived on time and seemed very professional, yet proved so highly dependent on technology that I rather lost patience with him. He disrupted my desk with his equipment – a laptop – and took me through a seemingly endless PowerPoint presentation, the bulk of which was clearly standard, when the whole purpose of the meeting was to link individually to my circumstances. The effect was the reverse of what was intended. While the charts shown looked good, their message was distanced from the client, and the proportion of the total message that came straight off-screen diluted the impression that the salesman made in a business where personalities and their expertise are crucial. Moral: in selling, technology must always *support* the personal presence.

Next, something good:

» *Good:* Prompt and effective follow-up can often impress. Again, recently I logged onto a Website, this time in the travel world. It worked well, gave me essential information, and allowed messages to be sent online. Not half an hour later the telephone rang. The company was overseas, but a UK representative wanted to help further. They knew something about me and were able to deal with the matter usefully. The link was still at a distance, but such contact should prove effective at making appointments where the next stage in encouraging a sale is a face-to-face meeting. In service terms this was impressive; in sales terms it achieved a real step forward in the overall process. Certainly such things would have been less easy only a few years ago.

In one case the organization took advantage of the technological possibilities and created a good effect on customers, perhaps a better one than in the past and certainly one in sympathy with modern expectations. The personal touch was still able to enhance the whole experience still more and the overall impact was positive. In the other case the technology worked, but seemed to have taken over. The salesman apparently felt that no individual consideration or tailoring was necessary, that everything was somehow "right" and all things to all people. He was wrong, and the impact of his sales approach was seriously diminished.

Overall, the morals of considering any examples such as this are clear:

» Use the technology by all means, and if you use it get it right and make it work. Technical failure in something designed only to support a presentation can nevertheless be taken as uncaring, unprepared (or worse), and dilute the effectiveness of the whole message.
» Match the technological elements to the real situation in client terms, always asking if what you do fits with what clients want in terms of service, manner, and handling. If there is not a good match, adjust the method or select some other way of acting.
» Always recognize that the technology can only ever support the personal input. If this weakens through reliance on the technology doing the job, then impact will certainly be diluted. Look at it the other way round in fact: personal skills can always enhance the message and the image. Use them, and use them wisely. Technology does not provide an excuse for not thinking about the best approach, every time.

SUMMARY

Things here are changing as you watch: "In the new digital economy, things are changing hourly and you have to be very adaptable, very flexible" (Kevin Kelly, *Wired* magazine). Fair enough, we know this. But selling is a frontline job; how it operates directly affects other people - clients. In this context you simply cannot embrace everything that is possible, nor can you experiment endlessly, inconveniencing people as you do so. The contribution technology can make to sales and selling must be carefully considered and even more carefully applied.

Whatever is done must:

» encompass a broad view of the business (not simply acting to save money or speed things up, but ignoring other issues, for instance);
» work effectively and genuinely do the job the clients want (and preferably do it better than in the past and than the competition can); and
» fit comfortably with the personal elements of the sales process.

Seeking opportunities here needs some priority, and is likely to remain an issue for a while, as the pace of change shows no sign of slackening and the technological possibilities are not just changing, they are becoming more complex.

The Global Dimension

The problems of providing a service across even a small part of the world market, and doing so in a way that achieves consistent quality and satisfies every client, are daunting. This chapter briefly describes the basis on which selling can take place:

» organizational options;
» global selling;
» cultural clashes;
» best practice.

''The world is becoming a common marketplace in which people – no matter where they live – desire the same products and lifestyles. Global companies must forget the idiosyncratic differences between countries and cultures and instead concentrate on satisfying universal drives''

Theodore Levitt

Undeniably the world is shrinking in the sense that it forms one big market; so much is interconnected and so many organizations now view the world, or a fair part of it, as their market. Organizations of all sorts are increasingly organizing to take advantage of this situation. For example, Unilever, which has recently cut its product list from over 1500 products to around 400, did so specifically to assist the job of marketing them on a worldwide basis. In services too this trend is visible. Citibank, the world's largest retail banking operation, tells its clients they can do business with it ''anytime, anywhere, anyway.''

The problems of providing a service across even a small part of the world market, and doing so in a way that achieves consistent quality and satisfies every client, are daunting. The ways of achieving this are beyond our brief here, though it is worth a few words about the basis on which selling can take place.

ORGANIZATIONAL OPTIONS

There are various ways an organization can organize itself to interface with a broad geographic market. Let us start with some broad considerations affecting services:

» *Who delivers the service?* For example, in my training business I can travel, as I do sometimes, and personally conduct courses in another country. I could also license other people, consultants in the country concerned perhaps, to run the course, and provide both materials and guidance so that they can do so. There are a wide range of options across the services spectrum.

» *How is consistent quality maintained?* If service deliverers travel, then this may present little more problem than working close to base. If other methods are used, creating and maintaining quality needs to be an integral part of the arrangement.

» *How is a consistent image presented?* Again, there are a variety of ways this might be organized, but the question needs addressing and marketing strategy must do this.

Thus different arrangements can change the way the sales process works. Selling may target intermediaries: selling a potential associate on a licensing arrangement for instance. Ultimately, selling may be done, on territory, by the staff of a distributor, an employee working for a subsidiary, by specialist sales people, or staff doubling up on the roles of delivery and sales (this latter is affected by the nature of the business).

Whatever arrangements may be made here, selling – and the methods it deploys – needs to be effective everywhere it takes place, and it is on this that we concentrate now.

GLOBAL SELLING

Selling a service in Singapore, Sweden, or Cincinnati demands the same care and essentially the same techniques as it does in Swindon. That said, potential clients want – demand might be a better word – a number of factors:

» *Convenience:* they want the same certainty of contact as they would get from a local supplier. It is no good pleading that distance makes this difficult, you simply have to organize for it somehow to meet requirements; and if there should be a slight shortfall this must be made up for in other ways, through the quality, exclusivity, or suitability of personal relationships, perhaps.
» *Understanding:* clients expect to understand. This may mean many things (translating literature, for instance), but certainly it means that selling must be in a language that prospects understand, and in some parts of the world this means something other than English. It means care too even in parts of the world with a "common" language: for example the 11th of January 2003 is written 11/1/03 in the UK and 1/11/03 in USA – a misunderstanding just waiting to happen.
» *Good businesslike relationships:* people the world over will buy from people they regard as "good people to do business with." The judgment that is made here, the service itself apart, involves many

things: liking someone, trust, professionalism, reliability, a tailored approach, going "the extra mile," and more. Some of the personal factors are unashamedly subjective; no matter, they still form part of the judgment. All this has to come over, despite any difficulties that distance, different attitudes, or different methods may introduce.

In addition, those selling services overseas must understand, and be comfortable with, the many cultural differences that can both confuse clear communications and stifle business relationships.

CULTURAL CLASHES

The actual task of conducting personal selling overseas demands some research and preparation. This could include finding local people to undertake the task; if not then things are more complicated. Even a brief selection of examples makes the point:

» *Understanding:* although English is to a large extent the universal language of business, those whose first language is English still need to exercise some caution in dealing with those for whom it is not. For example:
  » Speak a little slower than normal, though not so slowly as to sound patronizing.
  » Be careful and precise in your use of language: to ensure accurate meaning is transferred, consider restricting vocabulary a little.
  » Signpost clearly: that is, be sure to say what is coming and the nature of it – *let me give you an example... an important point is....*
  » Verify understanding as you go: again do not overdo it, but an occasional remark like *am I making that clear?* is useful.
  » Consider description carefully; the problem of bringing intangible things to life is even harder if language problems dilute understanding. Note: if discussions are being translated, special care is necessary and it is worthwhile discussing how it will be done with the translator ahead of the main discussion.
» *Making a start:* be particularly careful about the introductions and greetings; things like careful exchange of business cards (in the East), eye contact (not too long at first in the Middle East, and not with

women), and not flinching from a Russian bear hug can be important. First impressions last, it is said, and preparation must reflect this fact.

» *Personal appearance:* this is largely a matter of common sense. Decide what will be seen as smart wherever you are, and conform. If you are taken out, especially semi-socially in the evening, it may be worth checking what is appropriate in advance.

» *Manners:* this can be something of a minefield; you may need to find out whether you need to eat the sheep's eyes in the Middle East and you certainly need to know that it is rude to cross your legs and point your feet at someone in Thailand. Just the appropriate level of familiarity needs checking; the French for instance tend to be more formal than most people and Monsieur/Madame need to be used regularly. Equally you must not be unnecessarily offended by, say, the Chinese who can be very abrupt as a matter of course – *No, that's wrong!* – although without their meaning it quite as it would be taken if put that way in the West. Even seemingly sensible measures can cause problems: stressing honesty in Italy is taken as a sure sign that something devious is going on.

» *Body language:* the signs given in another culture may be confusing. In Bulgaria a nodded head means disagreement and nodding means agreement; in Korea too much smiling is taken as someone being pushy.

» *Humor:* careful! It may not travel; too much may be seen as inappropriately frivolous, but on the other hand you probably do not want to come over as too serious in some circumstances.

» *Timing:* attitudes to time vary around the world, and similarly punctuality has different degrees of importance in different countries; in Thailand people talk about "Bangkok time," meaning as close to a specific meeting time as traffic allows. More important, some cultures just take longer over some things. In America the culture is very much one of "getting down to business" fast; elsewhere, in the East, and in less "developed" countries for instance, preliminaries are important and time just to get to know each other a little is taken routinely.

Factors of many kinds may cause problems too. Take meal times: if you dine in Japan it is likely to be early (6/7 p.m.), with an Italian it will be late (9/10 p.m.). Getting this kind of detail wrong can offend.

As relationships grow, perhaps if you are meeting and doing business regularly, a wider set of circumstances needs to be taken into account and planned for – entertaining, for example.

Whether you are traveling to other parts of the world, or dealing with people who travel to you, some care in all these ways is sensible. Certainly it is important not to stereotype people or make assumptions; and this is easy to do when your experience of something is limited. In a people business this is especially important as judgments are being made that influence whether people will buy or not based on how your manner seems to characterize the service you sell.

Example – one country

The world is large and varied, so here, just to illustrate the range of things to be borne in mind, we consider one country, albeit one that is alien to many: Japan. Japanese business people tend to be well-traveled, are group oriented and rather formal in their dealings with each other. To get off to a good start when selling to Japanese people a number of things should be remembered. Do not overdo eye contact, shake hands only if a hand is offered to you (and do not try to bow in Japanese style, though a sincere nod of the head is appreciated), use titles with names, and make sure that careful use of language ensures understanding – checking as necessary. Business cards are much used (yours should have a Japanese translation on the reverse).

Details may be widely checked. You quote a delivery date and they will want to speak to those involved in implementing it to reassure themselves that it is seen as possible. The Japanese go to considerable lengths to conceal their emotions, hate losing face, and are uncomfortable if others (you) lose control, for instance showing anger or impatience. Respect and patience are to be displayed and any business transaction is, in part, seen as a pursuit of harmony.

Language will always need to be used carefully and you should not act immediately to fill silences, as taking a moment over things is normal. Politeness and consideration are valued, and personal touches (things like a thank-you note, or small gifts – you should ask permission before unwrapping if a gift is given to you) are seen as very much part of building relationships.

Specifically in buying: considerable detail is expected about any matter being discussed. An overview or seemingly vague or disorganized information will be read with suspicion as evasion. Good support material (what you see as sales aids) – anything from plans and graphs to summaries of details dealt with – is appreciated, indeed expected. As the Japanese will most likely deal with you as a group (it is unusual to deal with a single person), you must relate to the whole group, even those taking less part or less able to speak English (if that is the language being used). The differences here, certainly with a Western approach, are considerable, but even a snapshot like this is sufficient to show that a good deal of checking is necessary and likely to pay dividends.

Such detail, and more, is necessary whenever you focus on any specific individual market.

BEST PRACTICE

What makes for success is tailoring approaches to location and people (and, then, to individual clients – see Chapters 6 and 7). For example:

» Website management company Attenda can provide its service to clients around the world from offices in the UK and have multilingual staff available 24 hours a day. However, research showed that potential clients in Germany wanted to deal with a local company and with German people. David Godwin, vice president, reckoned "we are not big enough to buck the system," so a German subsidiary was set up and the people selling the service there are German employees of what is positioned as a local company. Whatever other problems they may have in a competitive field, no cross-culture problems should then hamper their sales success

» Similarly, Princtronic International, Europe's leading data-processing computer bureau, also has strong language capabilities. Its MD says "... despite English being the global business language our experiences in Europe still point to national languages being the preferred choice." Always, it would seem, selling services, in this case quite technical ones, is dependent on clarity of explanation and dealing with clients in the way they want to be dealt with.

» Another factor worth planning for is the circumstance in which selling takes place. This may be formal: a meeting or presentation. But it may present difficulties. I had a meeting with the publishers of this book recently on their stand at the London Book Fair. It was convenient for both of us, but I knew time would be short, distractions likely, and that my contact, who was doubtless seeing many people over the three days the fair took place, would have a lot on his mind. Preparation and execution have to allow for such things; when circumstances are disadvantageous it becomes more difficult to do justice to a case, and the intangibility of services becomes more difficult to balance. (In this case things went well, and you can read the result of our agreement, *Smart things to know about Becoming a Consultant*, which is now published.)

Finally, it should not be forgotten that matching client expectations in a global market costs money. If an American company wants to launch in Europe, it might well seek the assistance of the local office of whatever advertising agency it uses in the States. Selling would need to be done, certainly completed, in the UK. It would be normal in such circumstances for US executives to fly to Europe for meetings and presentations that aimed to tie down the business for the group. The actual and opportunity costs are thus high.

SUMMARY

Sales techniques are necessary wherever you sell, and the same core principles apply. It is the precise deployment – the mix of approaches if you like – that needs to match local conditions. But as selling always needs to match the buyer, this too is really a universal approach. Overall, however, success can be achieved if:

» sales technique is well chosen and deployed;
» service delivery (and image) is credible, i.e. however matters are arranged to deliver in a local market makes sense; and
» some consideration is made regarding local custom and practice.

Buyers will make some concessions to the fact that they are not dealing with a local organization (indeed your pedigree, so to speak, may be one of the reasons they want to talk). A few gaffes may be overlooked, but ultimately they will make a considered buying decision much as does any other buyer; selling needs the same sensitivity of approach wherever it takes place.

The State of the Art

You have to get what you do in selling right. It is axiomatic therefore that anyone selling services understands the process involved and applies suitable techniques sensitively and with some considerable precision. This chapter addresses key issues and gives a clear picture of what selling services involves, covering the following areas:

» first steps;
» preparation;
» using "product" information effectively;
» selling benefits;
» who makes the decision to buy?
» asking the right questions in the right way;
» the professional sales approach.

"It's the winning score, the bottom line, the name of the game, the cutting edge, the point of it all ... Prospecting, meeting people, building a flow of referrals, qualifying, presenting, demonstrating, overcoming objections ... they're all important. But, unless you can close, you're like a football team that can't sustain a drive long enough to score. It's no good if you play your whole game in your own territory and never get across their goal line. So welcome to the delightful world of closing. If you don't love it now, start falling in love, because that's where the money is."

Tom Hopkins, American sales trainer and author of How to Master the Art of Selling *(Harper Collins)*

As the quotation above makes abundantly clear, you have to get what you do in selling right; all of it. It may be unrealistic to expect a 100 percent success rate (so get ready for rejection too), but you need a good – cost-effective – strike rate. Every part of the approach and methodology that you take to selling to your clients must work. Any part that is weak can negate the rest and cause a negative reaction.

It is axiomatic therefore that anyone selling services understands the process involved and applies suitable techniques sensitively and with some considerable precision. The overall attitude and the expectation of buyers are dealt with in Chapter 2 and will not be repeated here. Suffice to say selling must *help people to buy* and be designed to prompt them to make what you consider to be the right choice. What approach does that suggest you take? The techniques involved are many, and success is as much as anything in the details; what follows is not comprehensive and should not put you off further study. It does, however, address key issues and give a clear picture of what selling services involves:

FIRST STEPS

The initial approach is vital; like any first impression, there are usually no second chances and no second prizes. So going about things the right way is key. However contact is set up (and this may come from a range of factors, from a prospect telephoning in response to a mailing, to some sort of cold contact), once it occurs, you have to make and carry through a personal contact. To do this successfully you must understand the potential buyers and make your contact both persuasive yet still always acceptable; in other words, not so "pushy" as to be self-defeating, yet sufficiently persuasive to create a good chance of the client taking the action recommended.

A persuasive approach mirrors the buyer's thinking. Selling must proceed with this thinking in mind and respect what the buyer is doing. Any sales approach that responds unsatisfactorily to any of the stages involved (see Chapter 2) is unlikely to end with an order. The buying mind has to be satisfied on each point before moving to the next, and to be successful a sales presentation sequence must match the buying sequence, and run parallel to it.

The two keys to success – to "closing the sale," as successfully obtaining a buying commitment is called – are:

» the process of matching the buyer's progression through the decision-making process; and
» describing the service, and discussing it in a way chosen to ensure that it relates to precisely what a (particular) buyer needs.

Early on, because the client needs to go through other stages, you may not always be able to aim for a commitment to buy, but must have a clear objective on which to close in mind. This may be to get the client to allow you to send literature, to fix an appointment to meet, or to provide sufficient information for a detailed quotation to be prepared. Whatever your objective is, however, it is important to know and be able to recognize the various stages ahead. With any client contact (by telephone or letter as well as face to face), it is important to identify:

» What stage has been reached in the buying process?
» Does the selling sequence match it?
» If not, why not?
» What is it necessary to do if the sequence does not match?
» Has a step been missed?
» Are we going too fast?
» Should we go back in the sequence?
» Can our objectives still be achieved, or were they the wrong objectives?
» How can we help the buyer through the rest of the buying process?

Naturally, as has been said, the whole buying process is not always covered in only one contact between the organization and the client. Every initial contact does not result in a sale, and neither does it result in a lost sale. Some stages of the selling sequence have to be followed up in each sales contact, but the logic applies equally to a series of contacts which may form the whole sales approach to each client. For a doubtful client, or a sale of great complexity and expense, there may be numerous contacts to cover just one of the stages before the buyer is satisfied and both can move on to the next stage. For example, selling exhibition space might involve only a few contacts, or conceivably only one; selling software to ensure a good fit with systems and intention for use might take many contacts over many months. Each contact has a selling sequence of its own in reaching its objectives. In turn, each stage is a part of an overall selling sequence aimed at reaching overall sales objectives.

PREPARATION

Planning the selling sequence to ensure that a persuasive approach is taken is key. Although only rarely does a contact take place exactly as planned, knowing and using the sales sequence and being able to recognize stages of the buying process are, however, invaluable. This can enable you to chart a course that matches the client's progress and allows you to stick as close as possible to your planned approach.

Adequate preparation is almost a magic formula. Yet it is only a formalization of the sensible maxim of "engaging the brain before the mouth." It may take up just a couple of minutes before you meet someone; it may involve sitting round a table with colleagues for a couple of hours thrashing out the best way ahead.

Whatever preparation may sensibly involve, the rule is simple – always do it.

Not least, it helps you undertake the core task of talking about the service better; and it is to this we turn next.

USING "PRODUCT" INFORMATION EFFECTIVELY

Identifying with the client, in order to recognize the stages of the buying process and to match them with a parallel selling sequence, must extend to the presentation of the core proposition. Nowhere is this more important than in the way you look at – and describe – your particular service.

"Product" knowledge (it always seems to be so called) is too often taken for granted by companies and by sales people. Sadly, experience of hearing hundreds of sales people talking what can sometimes verge on unintelligible gibberish, or at least is muddled and ill thought out, does not support this complacency. And it should never be forgotten that the difference between a good description – one that will help persuade – and something that proves inadequate, or actually dilutes the argument, may only be a few ill-chosen words.

You have to know what you sell inside out. More than that, you must know:

» the facts about it, how it works in detail, including the manner in which it is dealt with and delivered (and thus about the people that deliver it);
» what it will do for (or means to) clients; and
» how it compares with competitors (or other solutions).

Knowledge is not of itself sufficient. You must know how to put things over in the right terms and in a way that meets other criteria; for example, buyers may have a view of how long this should take, so maybe you have to encapsulate. The key element here revolves around the difference between features and benefits. But first things first.

A powerful clarity

The first principle of putting across product knowledge is clarity of explanation (which has the power not only to explain, but also to contribute to making your message impressive).

This may seem obvious, but because it can add so much to the effectiveness of a sales approach, it is worth a minor detour: see box.

NO ROOM FOR BLANDNESS

Selling needs precision. As has been said, usually there is one chance to influence people – and no second prizes. So whatever is said about your service must bring it to life, ignite the prospects' imagination, and bring some real description to bear. And this may even be what is done – to begin with. But it is sometimes said that practice makes selling worse. This means that the repetitive nature of selling – maybe with a large number of sales meetings being conducted each year – can make it become a tad tedious; and this is compounded by rejection. Sales people can begin to abbreviate, to ramble, just because they have been through things so often; or they become reticent and defensive, aiming for a pleasant conclusion – a "thank you" or an "I'll think about it" – rather than an outright "No." Whatever the reason, blandness creeps in.

No one sells anything that is *very nice*, *quite good*, or *rather worthwhile*. If there are no better words to describe it, forget it. Sales people can also be apt to use words that lack precise meaning. They offer something described as *personal service* (meaning what? That it is done by people – there's a blinding glimpse of the obvious), they say their approach is *flexible* (this page is flexible; again, what *exactly* is meant?), or offer *practical assistance*. Long moments of their meetings contain not a single adjective and, at worst, compound the problem with a plethora of inappropriate jargon and gobbledegook. I exaggerate (but maybe not too much).

All sorts of things must be done to make selling successful. But first it must inform, and do so clearly and in a striking way. The sad thing is that if someone asks "What's *personal service* exactly?" then what it means can often be spelled out, and may well sound impressive. More often this kind of question is *not* asked, and the overall impression retained is vague and lacks bite – and an opportunity may then be lost.

If you think – really think – about *how* to describe things, keep what is said fresh and make it descriptive, then results will be better. There is considerable difference between saying a material is *sort of shiny* and that it is *as slippery as a freshly-buttered ice rink*. Examine what you say about your organization, service, and way of delivering it and make sure it cannot be accused of being bland. The more complexity you have to deal with, the more there is to gain. If something expected to be complex is found easily digestible, then you surprise - and score points, especially if the description sparkles.

Of course, it is necessary to add to this, but the fundamental role clarity plays and the differentiation it makes possible should always be borne in mind.

SELLING BENEFITS

If you get into the habit of seeing things through the client's eyes, you appreciate that you do not really sell just "the service." You sell what people want to buy - not the service itself, but its benefits.

But what are benefits? This concept is key to successful selling and deserves a clear definition, one that differentiates benefits and their *alter ego*: features.

» *Benefits* are what products, promotions, or services *do for or mean to* the customer.
» *Features* are factual points about what it *is* or how it is delivered.

Consider an everyday product example: a man does not buy an electric drill because he wants an electric drill, but because he wants to be able to make holes. He buys holes, not a drill. He buys the drill for what it will do (make holes). And this in turn may only be important to him because of a need for storage and a requirement to put up shelving (and do so quickly, certainly, and easily). So, ultimately, the benefit of the drill can be described in terms of the ability easily to ensure safe fixing - given the need for storage and shelves. Similar statements for services perhaps demand even more care because they are intangible.

When this is realized, selling can be made more effective and it becomes easier to add a persuasive element to any communication. Selling is not trying to sell the same thing to a lot of different people using one worked-out standard approach, rather it is addressing and meeting each person's needs with personally directed benefits.

Benefits are what things sold can do for each *individual* client - the things they want them to do for them. Different clients buy the same product for different reasons. For example, a holiday may be for rest and relaxation or primarily to impress the neighbors.

Therefore, you must identify and use the particular benefits that match a particular kind of buyer and his or her particular needs. In the training which I sell, the actual skills developed (being able to make a better presentation, for instance) are obviously important. These must, however, link to actual tasks (the kind of presentations that must be made and what it is intended should be achieved by them), and other factors may also be important. Perhaps the organization is keen that a course motivates people, or has additional, more general effects, such as boosting their confidence or commitment. The complexities can mount up.

If we forget this, then the things that are important to a client will not always be seen as important from the seller's viewpoint. The result can, understandably, end in a conflict of priorities, with the sales person concentrating on what is important to him or her (their company, their service, and the need to sell). This can often come over with everything prefixed introspectively: *We are ... We do ... We have ...* (or interchanging with *I* or *The organization ...*), while the clients unsurprisingly takes their own view, one that reflects their own priorities and needs.

Any client is most unlikely to see things from the seller's point of view. Everyone regards themself as the most important person in the world. Therefore, to be successful, sellers have to be able to see things from the other's point of view and demonstrate through their words and actions that they have done so. Empathy is key, but it must show. Your chances of success are greater if you can understand the needs of the people you talk to, and make them realize that you can help them to fulfill those needs; and do so in a way that is different, and better (more appropriate) than competitors.

To do this necessitates the correct use of benefits. In presenting any proposition to a client, even simply recommending something in reply to a query, you should always translate what you are offering into what it will do. Often a company, and the people who write its sales literature, grow ''product-oriented,'' and ongoing development and change can reinforce this attitude by adding more and more features.

It is only a small step before everyone is busy trying to sell the product on its features alone.

Two examples emphasize the point. Many people need a "computer doctor" or trouble-shooter from time to time. Mine is Mark White (MDW Technology, a small company but deserving of a plug) who offers various services and could list all sorts of technical descriptions of what he does. Leaving technical competence on one side, for many of his clients, however, including myself, one thing predominates: communication. The benefit that he offers is that he takes the time and trouble to communicate with the layman. This gives him a real plus against competitors with equal technical skills and makes the understanding, trust, and peace of mind he brings to bear very real benefits. In a completely different field (*sic*), consider those in the agricultural world offering contract harvesting services (and blocking country roads with their enormous machines as they go from farm to farm). Apart from physically getting the crops in, the most important aspects of their service are surely timing and certainty. No farmer is going to hire them if, when his wheat is ripe, they cannot come promptly. What they say about this is at least as important as telling people about the model of combine harvester they use, and probably more so.

When competitive services become almost identical in their performance, it can be difficult to sell benefits, since all options seem to offer the same benefits. Choice then often depends on the personal appeal of some secondary factor. But even then, there must be emphasis on the benefits of such features, rather than on the features themselves.

WHO MAKES THE DECISION TO BUY?

To know what benefits to put forward, we must know what a client's needs are. And to know them, we have to know exactly who the client is. Very often, the client is the user – the person who will actually use the service. But frequently, the person who might be described as the direct client is a purchaser or a decision maker, someone who is not personally the user or will not be directly involved at least in many aspects of what goes on. This is most common in organizational purchasing, when a buying department is often responsible for the ordering, as well as handling the purchasing, of most of a company's requirements. Often it may be necessary to clarify this sort of situation. In incentive travel, for instance, a managing director may be involved in a major purchase, but not attend personally the sales conference for which he is helping to decide a location. Communications may thus need to be directed towards both the MD and the sales director (who will attend); and in each case be regarded as reflecting an understanding of the individual's particular role. Of course, if the conversation is with the sales director, and it is not known that the MD is involved, that is a problem; this kind of thing needs exploring.

In some situations a service provider may sell to an *intermediary*, who must be influenced so that they actually "sell," or recommend the service to final users, for example as a graphic designer might relate to a printer. Naturally, the requirements of the end-user will also be of interest to any intermediaries, but the best results are going to be obtained if sales people bear in mind the needs of both the buyer and the user, and the differences between their various needs.

Reasons to buy

Note that not all the needs will be objective ones. Most buyers also have subjective requirements bound up in their decisions, and perhaps nothing is bought on an entirely objective or subjective basis. Sometimes, even in technical areas, the final decision can be heavily influenced by subjective factors, perhaps seemingly of minor significance until all of the objective needs have been met.

Matching benefits to individual clients can make a successful sale more likely, for benefits must match a buyer's needs for agreement to be likely. The features are only what makes benefits possible: the contract harvester can offer to match the farmer's harvest time (benefit, one that in turn may give rise to others such as maximizing the financial value of the crop), because of the number and range of machines he has operating (features).

By going through this process for a particular service, and for segments of any range there may be, and matching the factors identified to client needs, a complete "databank" of benefit-oriented information can be assembled. Arranged and ready to be used in a way that reflects the client's viewpoint, it can be organized and documented if it is too much to hold in mind.

With competitive services becoming increasingly similar, more buyers quickly conclude that their main needs can be met by more than one supplier. Other needs then become more important. For instance, if a businessman needs to book a city center hotel, he is likely to find a number of them with similar facilities perhaps even within a stone's throw of each other, all costing practically the same. The deciding factors will then revolve around availability, and maybe more subjective factors like the ambience or the noise level in the bar. Details such as does it have a swimming pool, computer points in the bedrooms, or a movie channel on the television, also come to play a disproportionate part.

Sellers can look at the "features" offered by their organization as a whole and be ready to convert them to benefits to clients, in the same way as they can practice finding benefits for the full range of what is sold. Thus in an organization with a reputation for reliability, this can be used by the sales people to strengthen their case. Reliability is a feature, but clear, regular progress reports submitted during a market research project, delivered just the way the buyer wants them, may be a useful benefit of reliability and peace of mind. And worth mentioning in terms that spell out exactly what they mean – in this case perhaps, less checking, fewer problems, time saved, and a deadline or budget successfully met.

Every aspect of the company and its offering can, potentially, be described in terms of benefits. But it must not only be client-oriented and descriptive, it must also avoid being unnecessarily technical.

Jargon

A final hazard, which can destroy the external focus necessary during sales contacts, is jargon. This "professional slang," which can be useful of course when both parties are at the same level of understanding, comes in two main forms. Both can confuse clients:

» *Technical or industrial jargon:* sales people should normally let the client be first to use it. Technological complexities have already led to thousands of new words and phrases in business and industry, and introducing still more new terms seldom helps. But worst of all is the possibility that the client will not know what is being talked about, or will form the wrong impression, yet still hesitate to admit it (for fear of looking silly). So accountants should be circumspect about using financial terms, graphic designers printing terminology, and hoteliers should not talk about "covers" (the number of seating places a restaurant has). Abbreviations can cause particular problems.

» *Organization jargon:* it is even more important to avoid the internal jargon of a particular organization, for here the client will be on unfamiliar ground. There is a world of difference between someone saying: "Can do. I'll check the operational workload records on our CSD computer file and let you know shortly," and: "To answer that, we'll have to do a check on staff commitments and availability. The quickest way will be to ask for a computer printout which Head Office will forward to us. I can e-mail you later today with a profile of the suggested project leader and a possible start date."

Company jargon can have a wide effect, not only when used in selling, and even simple phrases can cause trouble. For example, deadlines present one area for potential misunderstanding. Promising "immediate information" might mean – internally – getting it to the client within a couple of days. But what if the client is in an industry where "immediate delivery" is jargon for "within eight hours?" They are almost bound to get the wrong impression.

Lack of unnecessary, or unexplained, jargon and clarity go together. Benefits are not just a way of producing bullet points; rather they constitute a route to benefit description which is client-oriented, clear and jargon-free.

The closer a description is to the clients' viewpoint the quicker and more easily they will take in a point that really means something to them. As a check, if you keep applying the words *which means that* ... to your descriptions, then when you can no longer add to the description you should have a powerful benefit. For example, someone selling an exhibition stand might offer:

» *the medium-size unit* (which is a simple form of jargon) – *which means:*
» *it is X square meters in extent* (a feature) – *which means:*

» *it is big enough to allow a dozen people on the stand at once* (better, this is a benefit of the particular size) – *which means:*
» *it will allow you to maximize the number of people you see during the exhibition and identify the maximum number of new prospects* (better still, surely this is exactly what an exhibitor wants to do?) – *which means:*
» *that it will be really cost-effective* (maybe a specific link to money can make what is said stronger still, especially if it could be quantified).

All very different from simply saying – *it's a good size.*

However, saying the right things, however descriptively and persuasively, is not all there is to selling; a critical stage is asking the right questions and listening – *really listening* – to the answers, and using these as a guide to how to proceed.

ASKING THE RIGHT QUESTIONS IN THE RIGHT WAY

Knowing how and why clients buy is a prerequisite to successful selling, and because everyone is an individual and wants to be treated as such, so selling must be based on finding out exactly what each person or organization wants, and why. In other words, questioning (and listening to and using the answers) is as important to selling as simply presenting the case. It is especially important with bespoke services where the precise way something is delivered must be arranged client by client (as in, say, consultancy or design). With no proper investigatory stage, a particular solution risks being seen as "standard," and whatever may be said about it, any credibility for it matching individual circumstances is lacking.

It is important, therefore, to start asking questions early in the approach, and asking the right questions in the right way is crucial. Two characteristics are important in getting this right. Questions should be primarily:

» *Open questions:* those that cannot be answered by "yes" or "no," but act to get the person questioned talking. They typically begin with the words: where, what, why, who, when, and how. Such questions work best and produce the most useful information (*closed questions* need using with care; they are useful to check simple factors, but can easily create something of a monologue).

» *Probing questions:* those that go beyond enquiring about the background situation, to explore problems and implications, and to identify real needs. They may start with phrases like – *Tell me about* ... or *Tell me _more_ about* ... If a series of two or three questions are necessary to get the information you want, so be it.

Without a doubt, good fact finding gives you a competitive edge: if you have found out more salient information than a competitor you should always be able to make what you say more pertinent to their situation.

The boxed paragraph illustrates this with a simple example.

THE QUESTIONING STAGE – EXAMPLE

A possible conversation between a travel agent and a prospect illustrates this stage:

Agent: "What areas are currently your priority, Mr. Export Manager?"

Prospect: "The Middle East is top priority for investigation but, short term, Germany has been more important."

Agent: "What makes that so?"

Prospect: "Well, we're exhibiting at a trade fair in Germany. This will tie up a number of staff and eat up a lot of the budget. Our exploratory visit to the Middle East may have to wait."

Agent: "Won't that cause problems, seeing as you had intended to go earlier?"

Prospect: "I suppose it will. With the lead times involved it may rule out the chances of tying up any deals for this financial year."

Agent: "Had you thought of moving one of your people straight on from Germany to the Middle East, Mr. Export Manager?"

Prospect: "Er, no."

Agent: "I think I could show some real savings over making two separate trips. If you did it this way, the lead time might not slip. Would that be of interest?"

> **Prospect:** "Could be. If I give you some dates, can you map something out to show exactly how it could be done?"
> **Agent:** "Certainly . . ."

This kind of questioning not only produces information but can be used creatively to spot opportunities. It accurately pinpoints the prospect's real needs and allows a precise response to them. Most prospects not only like talking about their individual situation, but react favorably to this approach. They may well see the genuine identification of their problems and the offer of solutions to them as distinctly different from any competitive approach that has been made, especially one that simply catalogs the services offered.

In the case above, it also allows much better demonstration of two factors that purchasers look for from travel agents. The first is *objectivity* and the second is *expertise* (in fact these are features; but getting the deal you want, cost-effectively and yet with the ability to make changes to the arrangement at the last minute without penalty, is certainly a benefit). The more this aspect of its case predominates, the more the travel agency is differentiated from any potential competition.

THE PROFESSIONAL SALES APPROACH

So far this section has highlighted key issues within the overall sales task. So, without going further than the intentions of this section allow, let us now consider just a few more factors that are crucial to individual success.

First, the basics: to be successful in selling services you must be able to:

» *plan:* you must see the right people, the right number of people, and see them regularly if necessary (sales productivity is as important as any other kind of productivity);
» *prepare:* sales contact needs thinking through – the so-called "born sales person" is very rare, the best of the rest do – and benefit from – their homework;

» *understand the client:* use empathy, the ability to put yourself in the "customer's shoes," to base what you do on real needs, to talk benefits and predominantly to lead with them;
» *project the appropriate manner:* not every sales person is welcome, not everyone can automatically position themselves as an advisor or whatever makes their approach acceptable, being accepted needs working at;
» *run a good meeting:* stay in control, direct the contact, yet make your clients think they are getting what they want (this is true of any sort of contact, including a telephone one);
» *listen:* a much undervalued skill in selling;
» *handle objections:* the pros and cons need debating – selling is not about winning arguments or scoring points; and
» *be persistent:* asking for a commitment, and, if necessary, keeping in touch and asking again.

Second, a variety of additional skills may be necessary to operate professionally in a field sales role. These include:

» account analysis and planning (a separate *ExpressExec* topic);
» the writing skills necessary for proposal/quotation documents to be as persuasive as face-to-face contact;
» skills of formal presentation; and
» numeracy and negotiation skill.

All of these (if you include liaison with colleagues as part of the first one) demand communications skills.

Before moving on, one last factor which influences the likelihood of sales success deserves a mention.

Holding and developing clients

There is an old saying that "selling starts when the customer says yes." This means that any company wanting long-term, repeat business must work at it – ensuring that the ongoing sales process continues to act to retain and develop business for the future.

Again, continuing the earlier example, the principles can be illustrated by reference to the travel agency example. The manager knows that in winning more business travel the overall objective is not one order, but ongoing profitable business from each customer if possible. Whether clients are retained, buy again, and do so in larger amounts is dependent primarily on two factors:

» *Service*: it may almost go without saying, but promises of service must be fulfilled to the letter; if they are not, the client will notice. A number of different people may be involved in servicing the account. They all have to appreciate the importance and get their bit right. If the client was promised information by 3.00 p.m., a visa by the end of the week, two suggested itineraries in writing, and a reservation in a certain hotel at a particular price, then he should get just that. Even minor variations, such as information by 3.30 p.m. and a slight price difference on room rate, *do* matter. Promise what can be done. And do it 100 percent.

» *Follow-up contacts*: Even if the service received is first class, the client must continue to be sold to after the order; in our travel agent example someone can:

  » Check with the client after his trip.
  » Check who else is involved in the next purchase. A secretary? Other managers?
  » Ask more questions. When is their next trip? When should the client be contacted again?
  » Make suggestions. Can the booking be earlier? Would the client like to take his or her spouse on the next trip?
  » Anticipate. Does the client know fares are due to go up? Can the client make the trip earlier and save money?
  » Explore what else the client might buy. Insurance? Incentive travel?
  » Investigate who else in the company travels. Other staff, departments, subsidiaries?
  » See whether you can distribute personal holiday information among the client's colleagues (with an incentive to buy?).
  » Write to your clients. Do not let them forget you. Make sure they think of you first next time.

A positive follow-up program of this sort, made specific to a particular business, can maximize the chances of repeat business and ensure that opportunities to sell additional services are not missed.

Such an approach brings us full circle, from the basis of persuasive contact (and the buying process explored in Chapter 2) to holding and developing clients' business on a continuing basis.

SUMMARY

The key to selling services is a conscious approach: one that brings an intangible to life, makes prospects feel involved, and makes them feel details discussed are tailored to their requirements. A sales meeting should be seen as *your* meeting. Take the lead, direct the action – run the kind of meeting *you want* (because it will help you sell as you wish), and which other people *find that they like* (and which preferably they find they like better than anything your competitors do).

With these essentials in mind, Chapter 7, In Practice, exemplifies them and adds further examples of how sales approaches can be made to work.

In Practice

This chapter is designed to exemplify the overall review of techniques that comprised Chapter 6. It starts with three case studies, and then covers the following areas:

» bespoke approaches;
» further good ideas;
» additional skills;
» organization;
» management responsibility.

"When you boil it down, your customers and clients use three criteria to measure you:

1 Communication
2 Service
3 Added value

How well you handle these three items is a reliable indicator of how long you'll keep your clients"
Mark McCormack, American sports consultant and
author of McCormack on Selling *(Century)*

This chapter is designed to exemplify the overall review of techniques that comprised Chapter 6. The comments and examples are designed not to reflect comprehensively the span of approaches and techniques involved, but to pick key issues that are both important in their own right and which illustrate thinking and action that can get selling services working as well as possible.

As has been said, selling is a dynamic skill. Quite simply, what works best is an approach that is well considered. It must never get in a rut or become repetitive and never reflect an erroneous belief that selling is a skill that can be perfected on a once-and-for-all basis. Rather it must be accepted that those who do best are those who never stop examining what they do and seeking change.

CASE 1: MEETING OF MINDS

Hotels have become almost a commodity product. In one sector there are often many choices for the buyer and all have similar setups to offer. This is especially true in the meetings and conference segments of their business.

Here is an example of sales approaches being adapted by focusing more tightly on the client. Venues of all sorts are at pains to encourage prospects to visit them – seeing is believing. However, sales people can have a problem arising from the nature of their business. Those working for a venue are usually proud of it; indeed, the better and higher quality it is the more they feel it "speaks for itself." As a trainer, I have so often been shown around a venue being considered for courses or events and heard nothing added to what I've seen by the sales person; indeed, sometimes you are seeing things at their worst: a dark, empty function room with chairs stacked in the corner.

Imagine looking at a conference space about as attractive as an empty aircraft hanger and being told *And this is where I suggest your wedding reception would best go.* The client reaction? *Forget it.*

Research done while working for the UK Meetings Industry Association led to the development of training that focused on this problem. It made clear that venue sales people were not in the business of selling rooms and tables and chairs; they see themselves more as being *in the business of helping people ensure their meetings go well.* Thus they need to:

» not just show but describe, and in so doing spark their prospect's imagination; the prospect should be able to imagine the meeting taking place there;
» assist imagination as necessary, for example using a portfolio of photographs to show how rooms can be set up differently for different events;
» convey confidence in service by the efficient way they operate (so that people really believe that things will work well);
» display knowledge and understanding about what goes on *inside* meetings, rather than just being able to set up for them.

This kind of approach embedded within the overall panoply of sales techniques can produce a more client-oriented and effective approach and improved results. As a result of this research, I have helped this approach to be applied by hotels around the world, including in Hilton, Holiday Inn, and well-known individual international properties such as the Oriental in Singapore.

Such objective thinking and attention to detail is to be commended; it might transform or modify the sales approach of any organization or individual.

CASE 2: DOWN IN WRITING

The kind of approach described above can be general or focused on very specific elements of the sales process. Another change, one that also occurred following research, concerns written proposals. These are an inherent part of the overall personal sales activity in many kinds of service business. In the professional services sector, a large international accounting group undertook a survey to investigate client attitudes to the style of the written proposals that the group used.

The survey focused on major projects where the financial value of the piece of work proposed was significant. Considerable dissatisfaction was found concerning the proposals. They were viewed as being too lengthy and also too formally written; in addition, they followed a long-established format rather too slavishly and were, as a result, not regarded as being well-tailored to individual situations and prospects.

Writing is not every sales person's best communication skill. It is, in part, a question of habit – *I suppose we write like we write*, as one of the partners said, actually exposing one of the problems. So, training was scheduled in the skills of writing persuasive documents, practice changed, and after some months it was wholly clear that the success rate of more recent proposals had improved.

Again the moral is clear. Every aspect of how the sales task is approached is potentially something that can be adapted to make improvements. As sales success is, in major part, in the detail of what is done, any aspect examined in this way can create improvement. This process is as much something that can be initiated by one individual as on an organization-wide basis.

Note: as an adjunct to this, and something that can also make a difference, I would mention controls. The firm above has a rule: it is unequivocally mandatory that anyone (at any level) sending out a written proposal *must* first have it read by someone who is not involved in the project. You get very close to this sort of task; two heads can be better than one – not just to check the spelling, but the logic, thinking, and explanation too. Many organizations follow this principle, and swear that it increases sales.

CASE 3: QUICK ON YOUR FEET

Whatever else may be said, especially about techniques, perhaps a disproportionate element of sales success in the service area comes from the way individuals conducts themselves. In "people businesses" the people are necessarily a major factor used by buyers in judging the merits of something. The more that the person is inherent to the service, the more this is the case.

While it does not negate the need for proper deployment of the techniques, if the people involved are quick on their feet and spot opportunities to demonstrate competence and maybe confidence and style too, then something worthwhile can sometimes be added to the mix.

A good example of this was the occasion, a while ago, when a colleague of mine of that time visited the huge ball-bearing factory of the SKF organization in Sweden. It was a sales visit to discuss sales training. As part of the company's ongoing public relations effort, as my colleague left he was handed a special printed card given to all visitors. This noted the exact number – many tens of thousands – of ball bearings that the factory had produced during the time since he had signed in at Reception. It made for a very impressive little piece of public relations. His response, though, was equally impressive.

With what I still regard as wonderful presence of mind, he borrowed a stapling machine from the receptionist and attached his business card, writing underneath the words – *But how many have you sold?* He put it in an envelope and sent it up to the marketing director whom he had just seen. It made quite an impression, and long after the sales training project, which was subsequently confirmed, was over, he was known within the organization as the guy who had dared to send back the PR card.

Ringing the changes in your communication and making a distinct impression is a creative process. You need to be constantly on the lookout for new customer communication ideas, whether they are one-off as above, or form the basis for new procedures. And to do this successfully you must always be close to the market and understand clients and their needs.

BESPOKE APPROACHES

One principle can dictate a great deal of action and achieve a great deal with clients. Sales in all its forms must relate well to the client, and for many kinds of service this means that the service itself is bespoke. Such can be a holiday package or a consulting project. The idea needs to show itself first in the way selling is conducted.

To see the value of this, consider an example of its lack. I received a written proposal recently from someone selling a service – a financial advisor. The proposal was wanted, expected, and followed a lengthy and detailed meeting. Suggestions were designed to fit my individual circumstances and seemed to do so, but, halfway through the document, my wife, Sue, was referred to as Margaret (and in case she reads this, no, bigamy is not a possibility!). Clearly the document had been adapted from another (presumably for someone whose wife was called Margaret). Now I have no reason to suppose that it had not been adequately adapted and it now surely matched my needs 100 percent. I also know that this adaptation is likely to happen and how easy it is to make such a slip. But, nevertheless, the error jars – am I now *really* sure that these recommendations are as tailored as I hoped? Perhaps not. Selling, as has been said, is a fragile business and nowhere more so that when what is aimed at being put across is a tailored approach.

So, selling a service is always made more effective by:

» an element of tailoring – include it where you can; and
» an inherent element of tailoring being well executed; small things, as above, can destroy the effect you want or dilute it dangerously. They can also enhance a meeting, a suggestion, a written proposal and more, making the message work harder and be more certain of doing the persuasive job you want.

Procedural danger

While I am on the subject of financial services, another danger comes to mind. The industry is heavily regulated (quite right too, there is no avoiding it). However, the way that many things must be presented can easily dilute both the clarity and the sales effectiveness of it – it seemed to me, for instance, that much of the length of the document referred to above was taken up with disclaimers of various sorts. Any such restriction simply means the sales approach must work harder. In financial services this is a considerable hurdle to get over. For others, similar problems can be home grown: internal procedures are not always as customer-oriented as they might be. Some such hurdles should therefore be removed, others are inherent and must be got around – just one more reason why a considered approach is so necessary when selling services.

A GOOD IDEA

The full flavor of what is necessary to sell services successfully is perhaps made clearer by some further examples, particularly to show the way in which apparently small details influence the client's reaction. For instance:

» *A link with the client:* the closer the identification established with the client the better. Clients want to feel the seller understands them and is focusing on the issues in a way that reflects their criteria and concerns. For example, in arranging a meeting at one hotel (a business that tends to be somewhat insular and concerned with physical arrangements), the sales executive referred to my need for a U-shaped layout as "putting everyone in the group in the front row." This is exactly how a trainer would see it – it is precisely *why* you have a U shape, for goodness sake – and immediately established the sales executive as more knowledgeable than is common. The feeling of sensitivity established lent additional credibility to everything else said. A sale was made. One phrase having this power is not unusual.

» *The power of questions:* all sales persons needs to know what their prospects and customers want. Asking questions is a necessary stage (see Chapter 6). But it must not be mechanistic; it must be made to produce real information and maybe the question *why?*, which can take matters to a deeper level, is the most important kind of question. Thus the courier company whose sales staff ask about *why* something is urgent can talk about the reason rather than simply about urgency or "good service." It is likely to be easier to sell on this basis. The customer does not just want it there tomorrow, he or she wants it in time for something particular that is important. It is like selling "*ensuring the biggest apology possible*" rather than just "*flowers delivered tomorrow.*" Get close to clients and they appreciate the difference it evidences in your approach.

» *Full description:* we all care about how much our insurance costs (say for house or car), but surely we care more about how it works - what happens when we have a shunt or a break-in. The small broker through whom I buy such insurance recognizes this. All brokers get good prices, and they tell you about the cover, but what sells me is their description of their role in an emergency, who will do what and how fast. Any service seller has to decide how to handle what to tell clients. What do you describe? What else do you describe and what do you give most emphasis to, short-cut, or omit? Recognition of the true issues and priorities – from the client's point of view – will pay dividends in selling intangible services every time. It pays to think about and really organize the methodology to be used.

» *Sales aids:* given the emphasis throughout this text that has been put on the intangible nature of services and the need in selling them to ensure that prospects are really made to imagine them in use, it is not surprising that sales aids are important in many kinds of service selling. For instance, there is not much less inspiring than an accountancy practice selling financial audit services. In one firm the accountants set out to overcome the problem of showing what you get. They prepared an example set of accounts in double normal size and annotated them in a second color. These could then be used at a meeting to show, especially to small and medium-sized companies, what the audit delivered, a process that highlighted key issues – managing cash flow and keeping the bank happy, for example – rather than just the statuary declaration at year end. This approach makes a good point. The task is not just to review what sales aids exist and decide whether any of it can usefully be shown. Rather it is to:

  » look at what points in the sale need strengthening;
  » create something that does the job (while also using anything that may already exist);
  » build it into the sales approach, so that it forms a cohesive part of the whole;
  » keep it updated and fresh; and
  » link it to controls so that it is used by everyone, whenever and wherever it is useful.

In so doing, not only is greater sales power brought to bear in a general sense, but such things can be tailored and used in different ways with different prospects.

» *Logic and sequence:* describing a service needs care or it will remain intangible. How you go about it is important and one important aspect of this is organizational. Nothing impedes sales effectiveness quicker than muddle – the "and another thing approach" that throws all sorts of unrelated facts at you in a desperate attempt to create sufficient substance to weigh in the balance. The way a message is organized is not a question of what is convenient to the seller. It needs thinking about in a way that will allow the client's logic to be reflected. My own accountant sensibly relates his description of audit work to the financial and tax year, taking people through what will be done, when, and what it will do for them. This service is actually regarded by many as an unfortunate necessity, an inconvenience, so a description that shows how it will fit the clients' operational pattern (rather than interfere with it) is the best basis for explanation.

A common thread here is the avoidance of any introspection – a focus on the client is what works best. Finally here, an example of how service situations – even negative ones as described here – can make subsequent selling easier and more certain; or not.

Airline cabin staff have a tough job; they do not meet people at their best (perhaps fearful, maybe jet lagged) but they are a tangible reflection of the airline's service. Two personal experiences make the point:

» Boarding a flight, I discover that not only is someone sitting in my designated seat, but that person has the same number as me on the boarding card – and was there first. The handling of this by the steward I approached, fearful of being bounced off the flight and with my business arrangements apparently in jeopardy, was impeccable. I was immediately assured that I would get on the flight, moved to another seat, and approached again as promised once the plane had loaded to check if all was well and to move me if necessary. A difficult situation handled promptly, politely, efficiently, and with recognition of the customer's concerns. With such an incident in mind, does it influence your behavior when making your next choice of flight booking? Sure it does. Thank you, Thai Airways.

» The reverse is equally true and perhaps even more powerful. My son, taking a bicycle to a sports event on a particular airline, was refused entry to a connecting flight on the same airline (who had agreed elaborate procedures to carry the bike) and charged a hefty additional sum as an alternative to being stranded halfway through the journey. All protests at the time failed to get the charge dropped, and it took eight letters of complaint over many weeks to get a refund afterwards. The fact that they relented in the end matters not. The people at the airport and in two of their offices that handled this matter ensured that sales would be lost, and did their public relations no good either. No thanks to Iberia. I will move heaven and earth not to fly with them again.

The nature of services makes all such things more important than in situations where a tangible product can be examined, and where its identifiable quality is apparent. With services, more of their "identifiable quality" comes from the way in which the sales side is handled, and the manner and style of the person doing the selling.

ADDITIONAL SKILLS

Selling services demands, well, good sales skills. One might define these as being persuasive communications skills deployed in meetings and often on a one-to-one basis. To leave it there makes the mistake of over-simplifying; there is more. Skills that go beyond this are just as important. In some cases it might be correct to regard them as "advanced" skills, in others any sale could be made by the application of one or more additional skills; or not. Such skills include:

» *Writing persuasively:* this came up in Case 2 above. To create fluent communication in writing, to make it persuasive and avoid an inappropriate over-use of jargon, an over-formal style (replete with sesquipedalians and galimatias – or, if you prefer, which you should, over-long words and gibberish), needs work. You need to know how to go about it, you may need to lose some long-held habits, and you need to practice. Getting this right is important. A little loose wording in a meeting can be rapidly corrected and may do no lasting harm. The same thing in a sales proposal is there in black and white, if not forever, at least long enough that it may come back and haunt you.
» *Making formal presentations:* somehow communication is different "on your feet," and perhaps also more difficult. It may not be fair, but it is a fact: with services, presentational performance is equated with the service to come. Make a poor presentation and people do

not say *What excellent ideas, pity the presentation wasn't better*, they are much more inclined to say *What a rotten presentation, I bet the ideas were not up to much either*. Again, this is a skill that must be studied and practiced. It is important wherever it is necessary, but perhaps especially so in areas where the "pitch" must exhibit creativity, as with those done in selling an advertising agency or design studio. Because prevailing standards are not perfect, it is very much an opportunity for some to shine, and to help the process of differentiation from competitors.

» *Working in a team (with clients):* this may not seem a major area of difference between working solo; after all, if you can come across well on your own, why not when working in tandem with a colleague? No reason, but it may stand some dedicated preparation or even a rehearsal. Teamwork in selling should be seamless; that is, one person should lead – effortlessly – and this need not necessarily be the most senior (look at the project and the client and see what batting order the logic dictates) and hand-over between them should be precise. There is no room for an approach that has someone saying *Well, I think that's all I need to do at this point; you were going to comment on timing, John, weren't you?*

» *Negotiation:* this is not the same as selling. Selling seeks to gain agreement, negotiation acts to decide the basis on which agreement is based. Often it involves complex balancing of the different variables: factors that can be organized in various different ways. In selling training, for instance, this can involve a long list ranging from the duration of a course and where it is held, through timing, staffing (who will conduct a particular program), to the many aspects of fee, payment, and terms. This is not in most cases an inherent skill. (Saying that lets me quote my favorite quotation, attributed to Annabel, aged six, and posted on the Internet, who said – *If you want a hamster, you start by asking for a pony*. This illustrates the bargaining nature of negotiation and the fact that some knowledge may be inherent, though for most of us it is something to study and learn.)

» *Numeracy:* sales made must be profitable. Anyone selling needs a certain fluency with figures, more so if selling routinely involves negotiation. All too often a more numerate buyer has been known to run rings round a struggling seller. Again, preparation can help.

» *Service delivery:* not only must sales activity be seen, in part, as an element of service, those selling must be knowledgeable about the service delivery. Indeed in many businesses the same people are involved in both tasks. This is especially true when expertise is involved: someone buying help building a house wants to talk to the actual architect; in such circumstances the job of selling cannot be delegated without loss of credibility.

» *Account management:* selling has both short- and long-term manifestations. In many businesses, working on a repeat or regular basis with a client is very much the intention. Account management is thus often ubiquitous. Creating the right relationship, maintaining and developing it, spotting opportunities along the way are all part and parcel of the process. It takes time, it must be planned, and it must be executed in a way that carries clients with you and delivers on their expectations. Just something as simple as judging frequency of contact must be just right. Leave contact too long and competition may take the opportunity presented to them. Make contacts repetitive or boring (the *Anything for us?* approach), rather than using issue-led ones, and clients quickly get fed up with it. Make contact too frequent and it becomes a nuisance and risks you being seen as desperate. Account management too needs organization, and perhaps investigation (see below).

To these might be added two further skills, first one that has implications across the whole spectrum of the sales task: that of being *creative*. This takes many forms, and an example from my own business, I guess the writing part of my work portfolio is a service, focuses on one specific sales problem, but illustrates an approach that can be applied more widely (see box).

Publisher Management Pocketbooks, having expressed interest in an idea for a book, then put the project on hold, seemingly interminably. Every follow-up I made failed to get through (a problem with which many will be familiar). A different approach was clearly necessary, something that would not fail to be noticed.

Finally, I wrote and sent the following, positioning it centrally and alone on a sheet of letterhead:

"**Struggling author**, patient, reliable, non-smoker seeks commissions on business topics. Novel formats preferred, but anything considered. Ideally 100 or so pages on the topic of *sales excellence* sounds good; maybe with some illustrations. Delivery of the right quantity of material - on time - guaranteed. Contact me at the above address/telephone number or let's arrange to meet on neutral ground carrying a copy of *Publishing News* and wearing a carnation."

I remember that I nearly did not send this, to someone I had met just once, and wondered, for a moment, if it was entirely suitable. I was pleased I did - confirmation arrived on the following day. So some creativity can pay dividends. (You can see the result of this in *The Sales Excellence Pocketbook*.)

Second, that of *keeping the approach fresh*, which is the antidote to allowing approaches to become unthinking, repetitive, and to proceed on "automatic pilot" (see box).

THE DANGERS OF "AUTOMATIC PILOT" SELLING

I have never seen a more dramatic example of selling on automatic pilot than that which occurred in a firm of architects for which I did some training work. They were pushing to take their clients up the scale - to work for larger organizations and on bigger projects. After a number of meetings and contacts they were short listed for a job with a major national charity (looking to build a number of residential training centers, I think). The final hurdle was a presentation.

Three senior people were to run the presentation, which was timed at three-quarters of an hour plus time for questions. They did put in time preparing: they met, decided who would do what in what order, and also spent time selecting slides to incorporate into the presentation, as showing the excellence of their previous work was an integral part of their pitch.

The day came and they arrived at the offices of the charity and were shown into the main conference room to meet, and present, to the managing committee. Intent on setting up their projector, they found their request to know where the electric socket was located was greeted with incomprehension. Then they realized what should have been evident to them throughout their contacts and planning: the charity was concerned with the blind. It transpired that most of the committee were blind. Two minutes later – without the slides – they made a bad presentation and lost the job.

If you can miss that, then you can miss anything. It shows just how routine and automatic selling can become – in this case slides were inherent, and no thought was given to it other than which to use.

Always proceed with due consideration and never allow the process, and habit, to dictate, even unwittingly, what you do. Every client situation calls for your best – considered – shot.

Each of these additional skills, and perhaps more, may need to become the stock-in-trade of those selling services. Certainly if you want to proceed to the top in this field it is likely that you will need to be able to deploy aspects of all, or most, of them. See if any of them relate specifically to your work now or in the future and whether, in turn, they stand some further study. There are *ExpressExec* volumes on several of these, including *Negotiation* (which I wrote also) and *Account Management*.

ORGANIZATION

Any sales person must be well organized. You have to see the right people, maintain continuity of contact, and use your time productively (and your client's – never get a reputation as a time waster). Here two further aspects of organization are mentioned:

» *Service selling/delivery:* the whole question of who does what and how things are organized is important and clear internal guidelines are necessary to direct action in a way that is most likely to maximize sales effectiveness. Often sales and delivery factors clash:
  » Who responds to a new enquiry, whoever is available or whoever has the best profile to deal with the particular prospect (and what if the latter is blocked out on delivery work – a lawyer might be in court, an estate agent out on a viewing)?
  » Who decides what happens in the above situation (and what criteria do they use)?
  » How is cross-selling handled? That is, how are wider opportunities to sell the whole range of services spotted and dealt with, and, most important, who precisely has overall responsibility for an individual client?
  » What about international links? How do you use a situation with a multinational prospect or client to get your Singapore office in touch with theirs?

There is a great variety of questions here; some may need policy decisions, and many can be actioned at the level of the individual. This is an important area and one that, though it is beyond our brief here, is picked up in the *ExpressExec* volume on *Account Management*.

» *Augmenting sales power:* there is still sometimes a feeling in some organizations that the way selling is done must be convenient. It may not be. What matters is that the approach is organized to maximize the likelihood of reaching agreement and doing so in a way that clients find acceptable. Concord Trust Company, who advise wealthy clients on their finances, find that many such people manage their finances on a rather *ad hoc* basis. They organize meetings that get themselves and their client together round the table with the client's accountant, lawyer, or any other professional advisor who may sensibly be involved. Matters can then be discussed with all the bits of the jigsaw being considered together. This is certainly much more difficult and time-consuming to arrange than just "taking the client out to lunch." But it is worth it, both in terms of what can be done and of perception. As Managing Director Henry Feldman puts it (interviewed in *Professional Marketing* magazine), ". . . when professionals do this they immediately transform themselves from railroad managers to transportation professionals in the eyes of their client."

The moral here is clear: selling must take place in whatever way achieves the objectives. Resenting the fact that it is difficult is not one of the options. Only occasionally can the reverse be made to work (see box), and always care is necessary.

THE BEST OF BOTH WORLDS

The financial advisor must have had something about him: I listened to his telephone call longer than I normally would and even asked him what the next step would be if I was interested. "You come and see me" he said. "You mean you come and see me?" I replied. When he said not, I declared an interest in how he worked and asked about it. His rate of strike was lower than many of his colleagues, but he wasted no time at all in traveling. His potential catchment area was smaller than it might have been (people had to find meeting him reasonably convenient), but his sales results were good. "Top of the league three years running" he said. Doubtless not everyone in his office could have made this work, but he did. Good thinking, tried, tested, and found to work. The productivity factor is obvious, but maybe people were also impressed by his confidence or simply intrigued by the approach. Differentiation is always important.

MANAGEMENT RESPONSIBILITY

The individual selling cannot control, and is not responsible for, everything. Management must set things up right. As an example: I recently telephoned Marriott Hotels to get a brochure about an overseas hotel. I got through to someone easily enough who took all the details, but who then said *You will need to allow for three weeks for delivery.* How long? This would have been after the person I wanted to give it to had visited and returned from the city concerned. When I expressed incredulity it was suggested that – *You phone the hotel direct* (an expensive long-distance call). I suggested that they telephoned and was then told – *We can only deal with incoming calls here*. Not very well, apparently. But the fault is not the operator's; it is in management's area. And the decisions made that create that situation must make life more difficult for sales people at every level. The moral is clear.

SUMMARY

Despite what has been said about success being a matter of getting many details right, two issues predominate here:

» *Selling services is a dynamic process:* there is no one right way (if only!), nor are there approaches guaranteed to work for evermore. Success comes most readily to those who accept the challenge this presents and constantly seek to fine-tune what they do to get it, and keep it, right for today.

» *A tailored approach:* this is a common factor. Working out "how to talk to clients" is not what is wanted; you have to work out "how to talk to *this* client," and the next, and the next. They are all different, so is your service, so are you. Approach every meeting in a way that seeks to reflect all the special and individual circumstances and which never lets people think they are in any sense getting the "standard spiel" and you are *en route* for success.

QUOTE

"Dealing with customers takes knowledge, time and patience – after all, if salespeople don't have that, they should look for another line of work"
Lee Iacocca, former CEO of Chrysler Motors and author of
Talking Straight *(Bantam)*

People are ultimately what sell services – people involved in service delivery, of course, but first and foremost people involved in selling. You, and the attitude you take to the sales process, are what bring in the business.

Key Concepts and Thinkers

Little of the jargon and technical terms used in the sales world are specific to selling services; however, key terms are given in the selling services glossary in this chapter, which also covers:

» key concepts;
» key thinkers.

"The question I always ask myself is, what would a customer, someone like me, want us to do?"

Charles Schwab, CEO Charles Schwab Corporation
(financial services)

Little of the jargon and technical terms used in the sales world are specific to selling services; however, key terms include the following.

A GLOSSARY OF SELLING SERVICES

Account management – The ongoing strategic direction of major clients' business.

Benefits – Those things that the service does for or means to buyers, rather than the factual descriptions of it (which are the features).

Buying signals – Signs that the buyer is at a stage of understanding and acceptance that permits closing to be tried.

Call frequency – The number of times in a year a customer is scheduled to receive regular calls; sometimes used to categorize customers and describe their relative importance.

Call plan – The statement of work to be done with customers, arranged with productivity and effectiveness in mind.

Client records – The basis of information, from contact details to buying record, that can be consulted in planning the next action with existing and past clients.

Closing – Action taken to gain a commitment to buy or proceed onwards towards the point where this can logically occur.

Cold calling – Approaches to potential customers by any method (face to face or telephone, say) who are "cold" – that is, have expressed no prior interest of any sort.

Cost justification – The part of the sales argument that deals directly with price, relating it to results or benefits and describing value for money.

Cross-selling – The technique of selling across, ensuring that a range of different services are bought by a client who starts by buying only one.

Competitor intelligence – The information collected about competitive products and services and their suppliers that may specifically be used to improve the approach taken on a call.

Ego drive/Empathy – Mayer and Goldberg's terms for, respectively: the internal motivational drive that makes the good sales person *want* to succeed, and the ability to see things from other peoples' (customers') point of view – and, importantly, being seen to do so.

Features – The factual things to be described about a service (see Benefits).

Field training – Simply training, or development, activity away from any formal setting, undertaken out and about on territory.

Gatekeeper – Someone who through their position can facilitate or deny access to a buyer (e.g. a secretary).

Handling objections – The stage of the sales presentation which is most highly interactive and where specific queries (or challenges) posed by potential buyers must be addressed to keep the positive side of the case in the majority.

Hunters/ing – The people or task of finding new clients.

Influencers – People who, while not having exclusive authority to buy, influence the buyer, through, say, their recommendation.

Kerbside conference – The post-call *"post-mortem"* and development session held when a sales manager is accompanying sales people in the field (which may often take place in the car – hence the name).

Key/major/national accounts – A variety of names are used here. First, measures vary as to what a major customer is; simplistically, it is only what an individual organization finds significant. A second significant factor is the lead-time involved. In industries selling, say, capital equipment, it may take many months from first meeting to contract and there is an overlap here with "major sales."

Need identification – The process of asking questions to discover what – exactly what – clients want (and why) as a basis for deciding how to pitch the sales presentation.

Negotiation – A different, though closely allied, skill to selling and very important in some kinds of business (*note:* there is another *ExpressExec* volume, *Negotiating*, which can provide a useful reference).

On-the-job training – Field training and development activity, often starting with joint calls with a manager.

Pie system – A structured way of managing the spread of customers and prospects around a sales territory.

Pitch – A formal presentation which is part of the sales process; may be general or in response to a specific brief.

Petal system – A practical way of organizing journeys to minimize time and mileage and thus help maximize productivity.

Proposal – Normally implies a written document, one including the price but more than a quotation – it spells out the case and most often reflects a clear brief which has been given or established.

Prospecting – The search for new contacts who may be potential clients; encompasses everything from cold calling to desk research to identify names.

Qualifying prospects – Research or action to produce information to demonstrate that cold prospects are "warm".

Rainmaker – A term most usually applied to those people who act to bring in new business, though not being in a full-time sales role (as with many in professional services).

Sales aids – Anything used during the sales conversation to enhance what is said; may be items, information (say a graph), or even other people.

Sales audit – An, occasional, systematic review of all aspects of the sales activity and its management to identify areas needing improvement, or those working well and needing extension; a process that recognizes the inherent dynamic nature of sales.

Sales productivity – The sales equivalent of productivity in an area, the focus here being on efficiencies that maximize the amount of time spent with customers (rather than traveling, writing reports, etc.): it focuses on ratios and touches on anything that increases sales success, however measured.

SPIN – Although this is a registered trademark, it is heard used generically – spin – to describe a customer-focused and questioning-based approach to identifying needs and selling appropriately in light of this knowledge.

Standards – Preset targets (absolute, moving, or diagnostic standards are all used) used to direct sales activity and to set objectives.

Team selling – Selling in partnership with others together in the same meeting; might be colleagues or collaborators.

Territory – The area covered by an individual sales person. It is usually, but not always, geographic.

KEY CONCEPTS

Three concepts are probably more important than anything else:

» *Services are intangible and cannot be tested:* this influences everything from the overall approach and the requirement for accurate need identification to detailed description.
» *Client focus:* sales approaches work best when they are tailored and seen to be tailored (conversely, an introspective or formula approach hurts service selling even more than it would other kinds of selling).
» *Benefits/features:* selling the benefits – what something does for or means to the client – may seem obvious, but it is also a major opportunity. Not everyone does it by any means, and when it is coupled with clear and creatively expressed explanation and description it allows a powerful case to be made.

These fundamental concepts underpin all that is said in Chapters 6 and 7 and details are not repeated here.

Beyond that, many other concepts have been coined. These too essentially reflect practical – common sense – approaches and, as such, are not revolutionary. The main examples include:

» *Strategic selling:* here the need to keep the long-term development of a client in mind is paramount (a whole approach based on the classic maxim *Don't make a sale, make a customer*); thus the link with account development is a strong one.
» *Consultative selling:* this assumes a focus on need identification, the advisory role someone selling services can have, or adopt, and uses this to create a well-tailored approach (this is sometimes called *advisory* or *solution selling*); it is axiomatic here that the role of sales is to assist clients' business success and profitability.
» *Conceptual selling:* here the focus is on description of intangibles (and again the requirement for need identification is stressed).
» *SPIN:* the Huthwaite Research description of service (and other) selling began with an emphasis on need identification (SPIN specifies the questioning technique needed to identify needs: Situation questions, Problem, Implication, and Need). It remains a well-packaged version of the core truths, one verified by the research base used to justify it.

All such concepts emphasize, quite rightly, the need to build good business relationships. The terminology of account management in the service sector may overlap with that of relationship management.

Note: a good many books and references about selling seem to focus on one aspect of the process, of which the most seen is Closing. Such do not normally pretend that their chosen technique is the only one that matters. Rather they use a particular way in to review and stress the importance of the whole process and everything that is involved in it. That said, it is a truism that all sales techniques are interdependent in the sense that you can do everything brilliantly and fail because you cannot close (or write a decent proposal or . . . whatever).

KEY THINKERS

The first true guru of the sales world was probably Heinz Goldman (who founded the Mercuri training company, and whose "road show" seminars were pulling in literally hundreds of delegates in the 1960s and well beyond).

Others have emulated this success in event terms, but this is not a field where individuals have significantly advanced the "theory" of selling to any significant extent. Rather there has been a gradual evolution of the sales process as more and more effective methods were sought, and better and more realistically behavioral approaches were gradually worked out (see Chapter 3 for more detail).

The way key thinkers have added to the total of knowledge here is to present and re-present the basics in ways that make it manageable and suitable to be deployed in the current environment.

Bear in mind the need for sales technique, especially that designed to sell services, to be directed in a way that both reflects the nature of particular clients and suits the personal style of the person doing the selling. Adopting the approach of any one technique advocate is not a likely recipe for success anyway.

SUMMARY

Much of what needs to be understood about the sales process is common sense. It is, as was said in the introduction, complicated because there are a good many techniques and approaches to keep in mind, and to orchestrate in your sales conversations. None of the key thinkers referred to here, or indeed less eminent commentators on selling, can provide a magic formula. However, because of the dynamic nature of the process, an ongoing study, looking at what must be done and what works in different ways, is useful – not least because approaches do change over time. Services are different, but you should not shut your eyes to material about other sorts of selling, as there may well be lessons to be learned from there too.

THE ULTIMATE KEY THINKER

Ultimately, the best coach is always with you. If you can develop the habit of reviewing what you do – literally meeting by meeting – and be open and objective about what goes well or less so, about what works and should be further utilized or what does not and needs discarding, then your selling will constantly improve. It will also better reflect client needs and expectations because it will constitute a methodology selected for today, rather than the habitual approaches of the past, which, however well they used to work, may – will – become outdated.

POSTSCRIPT

Pausing while writing this, I went out for lunch and called into an estate agent's (an individual office of a chain) to get details of a new development the sale of which they were handling. Nice brochure, very polite, a little sensible information volunteered ... but I was not asked a single question; not even who I was. So, no follow-up possible there. Surely it is common sense that certain things are an absolute reflex. Success in selling is, in part, a state of mind – it must be a positive one.

Resources

Countless words have been written about the subject of selling services. This chapter identifies the best selling services resources:

» defining the job;
» books;
» training films;
» professional bodies;
» magazines.

"It is a nuisance that knowledge can only be acquired by hard work"

W. Somerset Maugham

What can you do to add power to your selling arm, and what outside resources can assist? What follows is unashamedly a rather disparate group of things: sources of ideas, information, and inspiration varying from films to professional institutes and Websites.

Before getting into these, there is one point to make. As was said at the end of the last chapter, you are your own most effective coach. As a totally biased plug, I would mention the companion *ExpressExec* volume *Self Development for Sales People;* worth a look, I would suggest (but if an author cannot say that in a book about selling, where can he?). Back to resources.

DEFINING THE JOB

The selling job, like many others, has evolved over time. Most sales jobs have a great deal more about them than just being "to sell." If you want a clear overview of what today's sales jobs entail you can do worse than look at a research study titled *The Future of Selling*. This is a report published late in 2000 by Quest Media Ltd (the publishers of the journal *Winning Business*) in association with the Institute of Professional Selling and consultants Miller Heinman Inc. This is an interesting research study, more so because the area is rarely researched. It reviews current practice and looks to the future, examining: the changing sales role, customer expectations and beliefs, and the whole way sales teams are organized, staffed, rewarded, and managed.

Key findings indicated that:

» Customers are becoming better informed and more organized, demanding, and sharp in their dealings with sales people (with the Internet being used to a significant extent for pre-buying research.
» Technology is having, and will continue to have, an effect on sales activity: most dramatically it is replacing sales people with electronic, impersonal, buying, though this is not affecting large numbers of business areas. The dynamic nature of this area is evidenced by the

uncertainty respondents reflected in their forecasts of what other influences are becoming important.

» Recruitment is a perpetual challenge, as is retention.
» CRM is becoming a more widespread basis for many customer interactions, and creating a more formal basis for them.
» Training remains a constant need (and more of it is being done, and the range of ways in which it is done are also increasing) as the level of competency of sales people is seen as key to success.
» Reporting takes a high proportion of working time – reducing sales people's time spent face to face with customers; this despite the increasing computerization of data collection and reporting systems.

Sales management, its practice, manner, and style, is seen as significant to success. On the one hand, the increasing professionalism of the sales role and the broadening of sales people's responsibilities in response to market changes heighten the role and managerial skills sales managers must have. Your own level of success is certainly affected by the kind of managers for whom you work (whatever they may be called) and, to be honest, the kind of relationship you create with them. They should be a source of support, inspiration, and learning. If they are not, you may need to ask yourself a few questions.

It is a valuable study that deserves to be repeated on a regular basis. It is expensive to buy, but must be in many business libraries; worth a look.

Link

As "Winning Business" below.

BOOKS

There are more books about selling than you can shake a stick at. They fall primarily into three categories:

» Those that are personality based – the gurus – comments on selling. Such include:
    » *McCormack on Selling* by the American sports agent Mark McCormack;

- » *Close that sale* by the British motivational speaker and trainer Richard Denny; and
- » *Making major sales*, by Neil Rackham (of Huthwaite Research and SPIN fame).
- » Those that present essentially workmanlike expositions of the sales process and how to go about it, such as my own *101 Ways to Increase Sales* (Kogan Page) which reviews the process in bite-sized sections.
- » Those that look in detail at selling, or aspects of it, and tend to concentrate on the behavioral aspects of the process. Such include: Mack Hanan's book *Consultative Selling*. This sets out a total approach to selling, one that assumes that a constructive business relationship, partnership even, is necessary and that what is being sold genuinely solves problems and assists the client organization to be successful.

All can be useful, though which is most useful is likely to be as much a question of what suits you and your style as anything else.

Every particular specialization of selling, from telephone selling to dealing with major accounts, is also well documented. Perhaps the answer is to read something regularly; it will be a while before repetition becomes a real problem, although most books are essentially looking at similar techniques, albeit presented in a variety of different ways.

Beyond this, there are books which present a more complex (though sometimes frankly over-engineered) view, with titles reflecting ideas such as conceptual selling. These are in many cases heavily behavioral. They may extend your view of things somewhat but need to be more carefully chosen than simpler texts and to focus on your particular interests.

As an additional thought, it may be worth having a look at books designed for buyers. Understanding how it is suggested they go about things is, at the least, interesting. Only one publication comes to mind that is designed to instruct buyers in how specifically to deal with sales approaches and, though it is not designed for service situations and is a few years old, this could still be worth a look: *Buying from Publishers' Representatives* (The Booksellers Association).

Finally, there are a number of books that look at selling particular services. There cannot be one for every service field, but ones that are, or regard themselves as, very different from the main run do tend to have literature devoted to them. Among them are:

» *Maximising Hospitality Sales* (Continuum) by Patrick Forsyth – for those in hotels and other venues such as conference or training centers;
» *Selling Skills for Professionals* (published by the conference company Hawksmere plc) by Kim Tasso – a very practical and detailed review for those selling professional services.

Another route to information is through books on marketing of services. Some are light on coverage of sales, others may have a useful chapter. Some, for example *Marketing Professional Services* (Kogan Page/Institute of Directors), are specific to particular service sectors. The most prolific marketing guru, Philip Kotler, has targeted several service sectors, with books including: *Marketing for Health Care Organizations, Marketing for the Performing Arts*, and *Social Marketing* (that is, for non-profit organizations such as charities). Other authors will help put selling in a broader context, for instance American guru David H. Maister who has written extensively about professional services, for instance in *Managing the Professional Service Firm* (Simon & Schuster).

TRAINING FILMS

Some readers in full-time sales jobs may be familiar with some of the many training films used in sales training. There are many producers (Video Arts Ltd – producers of what were universally known as the "John Cleese films" – are perhaps best known, though the actor is no longer associated with them; they can be accessed on www.videoarts.com) and they cover almost every aspect of selling.

If you can get to see such things, they can be useful and the best encapsulate aspects of selling in memorable, and often humorous, ways. They are quite expensive to buy or even hire, but ask your manager, attend previews, or seek them out in libraries or professional bodies.

One warning: films are often designed to be the core of a complete or mini-training session. It would be wrong to think that everything you need to know about a topic is contained within the 20/30 minutes of a short video. So, you may do best to link any viewing to something else to fill out the picture (a meeting with a mentor, reading a book, whatever).

PROFESSIONAL BODIES

The main body in the UK concerned with the sales area overall and sales people is **The Institute of Professional Sales**. This describes itself as follows:

The vision of IPS is to create an Institute which recognizes both the achievement of professional qualifications and the value of experience.

Its aim is to bring together the knowledge of academia, the skills of training organizations, the experience of practitioners with the motivation essential for all selling roles.

The objective of IPS is to raise the profile of sales people and to gain recognition for the sales function. In addition, we want to create a very clear training path for those coming in to sales.

Additionally, we wanted to provide events and networking opportunities and to define and evolve "best practice" in sales.

Successful selling is essential for any business and the Institute of Professional Sales aims to make selling an accurately defined science rather than just an acquired art. All the qualifications are based on the National Standards together with the real life experience of first class trainers.

The corporate benefits offered are that IPS will recognize training by external companies and help to raise the profile of the sales profession within those companies. IPS is dedicated to raising standards of best practice, is compatible with Investors in People and encompasses many industry leaders.

Individual benefits of joining IPS include use of the designatory letters, advice on career development, *Winning Business* magazine, an active Regional Events program and access to the Information and Library Service.

For more information on the IPS, please visit the website on: www.iops.co.uk or email the Institute on: johnmayfield@iops.

co.uk. It can be contacted at the same address as The Chartered Institute of Marketing, that is Moor Hall, Cookham, Maidenhead, Berks SL6 9QH Telephone 01628 427500, of which it is a part.

Other useful bodies have, because of their prime role, an inevitable overlap with sales. The first two are concerned exclusively with professional services:

The PM Forum
Warnford Court
29 Throgmorton Street
London EC2N 2AT
Tel: 020 77869786
www.pmint.co.uk
This networking group is linked to the journal Professional Marketing and has a focus on the marketing of professional services (and a sister group concerned with financial services marketing).

The Professional Services Marketing Group
PO Box 353
Uxbridge
UB10 0UN
Tel: 01895 256972
This is similar to The Marketing Society, but is exclusively for those working in the professional services sector (with firms such as accountants, lawyers, surveyors, architects, consultants, etc.). Their main activity is through member meetings of various sorts. There is a Website: www.psmg.co.uk.

MAGAZINES

There are many magazines covering the marketing area, either from a general perspective or with a focus on one specific sub-section of marketing, but only a few are of significance and focus on sales.

Winning Business
Quest Media Ltd
9 The Leathermarket
Western Street
London SE1 3ER
Tel: 020 73781188

This is probably the most useful magazine in the field, and not only because I write for it regularly! The publishers describe it thus:

"Winning Business" is a leading edge, bi-monthly magazine published in association with the Institute of Professional Sales, targeted at and read by senior managers within organizations that have responsibility for customer-facing aspects of their business, such as sales, marketing and customer service. The uniqueness of the publication relates to the fact that it is the only "how to" focused magazine in the UK that provides senior managers with advice, guidance and inspiration to help them win more business.

The editorial of the magazine is designed to be of interest to any business leader interested in finding, winning, retaining and growing business.

The benefits of publishing a magazine that has many of Europe's top business experts writing for it have enabled the editorial team to build a framework of key business principles around which content is developed. This approach means looking at the subject of how organizations find, win, retain and grow business from three very specific areas, people, processes and technology.

The magazine aims to explore how organizations develop and evolve their people and their processes to increasingly meet and exceed the needs and expectations of customers whilst using technology to enable the changes and developments they wish to make. The other key principle is to encourage organizations to increasingly integrate the different functions of the organizations, particularly their sales, service and marketing operations in order to improve the consistency and the quality of the experience for the customer.

This consistent framework enables the magazine to build on and broaden the range of issues and subjects it addresses whilst continuously questioning the validity of any new ideas and concepts against its core principles.

To achieve its objectives, *Winning Business* brings together global experts on sales, service and marketing. They write to a tight brief, resulting in easily accessible, knowledgeable and authoritative editorial that consistently shows its readers how to succeed in their efforts to find, win, retain and grow business with their profitable customers.

The magazine is packed full of advice, ideas, best practice and research identifying and exploring the best and most effective ways for organizations to constantly improve their performance. By providing a reader-friendly package of high quality, interesting, practical, and thought-provoking advice in an expertly written, well-designed format, the magazine captures the attention of senior business leaders, influencing the opinion formers.

This is not specific to services, but still well worth a look.

» *Sales Director*
  This is also useful and has very much the style and format of something like the journal *Management Today*.
  www.saleszone.co.uk
» *Sales & Marketing Management*
  The main US magazine on the subject, broader than solely sales management and containing useful material.
  www.salesandmarketing.com
» *Sales & Marketing Professional*
  This is the journal linked to the Institute of Sales & Marketing Management. Somehow this has always remained in the shadow of the main institutes; its base is sales, but it seems to think marketing is sexier and positions itself "higher."

All the above are specific, but it is worth bearing in mind that, as selling is an essential part of the marketing mix, marketing journals feature articles on selling and sales management from time to time. The Library at the Chartered Institute of Marketing will produce lists of recent articles on request, though there is a charge to non-members. Complex aspects of selling are catered for via various Websites, for example www.SoftTools.net (this focuses on sales planning and provides a platform to assist with the task) and www.speakingconnection.com (an American site for those interested in sales planning).

Finally, for a general overview of marketing issues (which inevitably touches on sales and business development as a topic), the CIM journal is worth noting:

Marketing Business
Exmouth House
3-11 Pine Street
London EC1R 0JH
Tel: 020 79235400

FINALLY: THE ULTIMATE RESOURCE

It has been clearly stated that selling is a dynamic process. It never settles and the challenge is to sell in a way that works today, and in another way that works tomorrow. It needs to be varied client by client and circumstance by circumstance. Training, in all its forms, may help you develop skills and keep them up to date. So can reading about it, liaising with a mentor and more, but such things are essentially transient. The one thing that is always available for comment and which can act as a catalyst to development can be stated in a word.

You.

At the risk of being repetitive, the people who excel at selling certainly tend to have one thing in common: they recognize that success comes through working at it; and they do just that. They observe, analyze, and adjust. They experiment. They review what they have done – with an objective, rather than a defensive eye – and see what they can learn from it and what they can do differently, and what they can build on because it worked well.

No one gets a sale every time, certainly not in the challenging and intangible world of services, but those who adopt a consistently conscious approach, and who fine-tune everything about their approach, tend to get the best strike rate. Everyone is in a position to take advantage of this development route (start by checking out the *ExpressExec* title *Self Development for Sales People*).

Ten Steps to Making Selling Services Work

This chapter summarizes key aspects of what makes for success in selling services:

» Selling is part of marketing.
» Selling must be client-oriented.
» Selling must reflect the buying process.
» Selling demands preparation.
» Selling must be delivered in an appropriate manner.
» Selling must incorporate effective need identification.
» Selling must use memorable and creative description.
» Selling must be benefit-led.
» Selling is a complex process and must be managed.
» Selling effectively must take a long-term view.

"A salesman has to use his imagination, deliberately and consciously, to think up just what little things he can do to be helpful to each customer. Every case calls for different tactics. That fact helps explain why aptitude testers maintain that the two traits most needed for success in selling are an objective personality and creative imagination."

> *Alex F Osborn, author* Applied Imagination: Principles and
> Procedures of Creative Thinking *(Scribner)*

If I knew one key magic formula that always guaranteed sales success I would not be writing this; I would be rich and retired. There is, as has been said earlier, no magic formula. There are, however, a variety of things, techniques, approaches that have a disproportionately important influence on success. Some such have been mentioned throughout the text. Remember that success in selling is largely in the detail, and that it is a fragile process. Here, without intending to sideline other issues, we summarize key aspects of what makes for success in selling services under 10 main comments.

1. SELLING IS PART OF MARKETING

Sales activity must not take place in isolation. It *is* an inherent part of marketing. Thus sales people must:

» Recognize that clients see, and experience, sales in this way. For example, they may know something of an organization ahead of a sales meeting (from promotion and advertising, amongst other things); they may have checked out competitors, visited a number of Websites, and more. They expect what happens through the sales people to reflect, maintain, and extend any good image that may have been projected. They expect specific promises made through other media to be kept. If your Website tells people *A half hour briefing will give you all you need* – then it had better do just that.
» Act and talk in a way that gels well with other activities and messages.

This presupposes that marketing activity is conducted in a way that sees personal selling as an integral part of the way the organization interrelates with its clients. So advertising may need to reflect the fact that prospective clients will need to see a sales person as part of the process that is necessary if they are to make a sensible buying decision. Mismatch here just causes problems and jeopardizes potential sales. If a sales person promises further information, then contacts the office to prompt the action and then there is a delay, the potential client will see this as an inefficiency of the sales person (and the organization).

Sales people have a responsibility to spot any such occurrences (and they can come from many areas) and communicate about them to ensure they are corrected. Good management is alert to such intelligence and will ensure that things run smoothly and that nothing is allowed to dilute sales effectiveness.

2. SELLING MUST BE CLIENT-ORIENTED

Selling, to repeat, is not something that you do *to* people. It is an interactive process that must, as much as anything, reflect the client end of the relationship. This means specifically that:

» People's needs must be accurately identified. Only if you know what their situation (it might be a problem or an opportunity) is can you address it; moreover, if you address it better than competitors then this is the very best method of differentiating yourself and your organization.
» Sales approaches must respect the individuals on the other end. Are they experienced, knowledgeable (or not), are they worried or confident? Sales conversations must not just incorporate such information and do so specifically, but also *be seen* to do so. Displayed empathy scores points.
» Above all, especially in selling bespoke services, a sales approach must *not* appear standardized. People must feel you are interested in them, addressing their specific situation, and that what you say is *for them*, not just what you always say to everyone.

A conscious focus on the client will help direct the entire communication in the right kind of way, giving it bite and giving it an edge.

3. SELLING MUST REFLECT THE BUYING PROCESS

This picks up from point 2. Here what is advocated is not a general client orientation but a reflection of the whole process that a client is going through in making a decision. In the same way that in boxing or judo you "go with the attack," here you will do better following the client's inclinations (though perhaps modifying and imparting particular emphasis to them) rather than fighting against them. The thinking process set out in Chapter 2 really does constitute an effective basis on which to proceed. If you get out of kilter with prospects, then not only will they not see the relevance of what you are saying, they will resent it.

When I changed my car recently, I talked to three dealers (looking at cars in broadly the same bracket). I was not asked a single question by any of them. Amazing! How can you sell a car if you do not know whether the potential buyer is married, has children or a dog, how many miles he drives in a year, and more? I was offered lots of information, but it completely lacked any credibility – it was the standard spiel. This is a dramatic example, from another sector, but makes a good point. The logic dictates that the customer expects to be asked questions, and for the presentation to be based on the answers. Any aspect of the client's buying process that is ignored risks failure and the likelihood that what they want will be better satisfied elsewhere.

4. SELLING DEMANDS PREPARATION

You cannot wing it. Even the best and most experienced rarely wing it (though they may make it look a little like they do). Success comes from sound preparation. The first rule is simple – *you always prepare*. What actually needs to be done, however, may vary considerably.

You may only need a couple of quiet minutes before going into someone's office. You may need to sit down with one or two colleagues for a couple of hours to thrash out the best way ahead. You may not be able to prepare (as in a retail situation when the client walks right up and the transaction is under way). In the latter case you need to be prepared: you can think in advance about the type(s) of transaction that may occur and be ready for most of them.

You may need to make notes, you may need alternative strategies, or you may want to rehearse (for a major sale). You *do* need to do something. Consider exactly what is needed in every situation, do it, and you automatically increase your chances of success. You cannot predict exactly what will happen, you still need to be quick on your feet, but you will be better able to cope with whatever may come your way if you are prepared.

5. SELLING MUST BE DELIVERED IN AN APPROPRIATE MANNER

Selling services needs a soft approach (*not* lacking in persuasive power) but not weak either. The power – projection – that you bring to bear is important. You need confidence, authority even, certainly people must believe you have the position, personality, and profile to be credible in your role.

Empathy is the other key attribute. You need to see things from other people's point of view and *be seen to do so*. Good empathy balances the powerful approach you want to bring to bear, it softens sales techniques that would otherwise be seen as "hard sell," and makes what you do acceptable as well as appropriate.

This is especially important when there is an element of advice inherent in what you are doing; and there is in many service selling situations, from selling travel to consultancy. Advice must seem soundly based. It must not simply and obviously be what you want and what is best for you. The right blend here is worth working at. Think about how your kind of clients might best want you to come over and try to match their expectations to some extent. Do not leave out the edge you want, but remember that if what you do is not acceptable it will quickly be rejected as your prospect moves on to talk to a competitor.

6. SELLING MUST INCORPORATE EFFECTIVE NEED IDENTIFICATION

Selling is not just about telling – describing – things to people. Success has at least as much to do with asking questions. So:

» Think about areas to question and plan how to phrase matters clearly (not least so that you can get the information you want quickly and the process does not become like the Spanish Inquisition).

» Establish and agree that questioning is necessary (you do not want it to distract or worry people – the logic of the approach should be clear).

» Listen – as in LISTEN – to, and note if necessary, the answers.

Then your presentation can be tailored around you client's exact situation. The principle here is the same whether the circumstances only permit a couple of quick questions or if you can take half an hour really to establish details (what they want, and *why* they want it). Always, good needs-identification puts you in a position to make a better, and better targeted, pitch and differentiate more easily from competition.

7. SELLING MUST USE MEMORABLE AND CREATIVE DESCRIPTION

There is a danger with any kind of selling that what is said becomes routine, repetitive – and dull. The seller starts to abbreviate a little (because he or she has heard it all before) and the best possible case is no longer made.

There are principles to be followed here:

» Remember that unexpected clarity (especially if something is expected to be complicated) delights the buyer – you need to communicate and, with services especially, to ignite people's imagination. This is a real opportunity to shine (and again to differentiate).

» Think about the best way of putting things, and do not let the way you talk about something become stale.

» Keep what you say up-to-date, correct, and fresh, and make sure it is in "the client's language" (and remember too much jargon can deaden any description).

» Bring it to life. Avoid bland language – no service is *quite* (or even *very*) *good* – and avoid imprecise words like *flexible* which attempt to be descriptive and fail (what does flexible mean, for goodness sake? If you are reading this in book form, then this page is flexible). Work at a description to create something clear and memorable.

It is one thing to say something is *sort of shiny* (wet fish?). It is better to say it is *as smooth as silk* (which certainly conjures up a more precise image), and better still – and more unmistakable and memorable – to say that it is *as slippery as a freshly-buttered ice rink* (see Chapter 6).

Language is the most powerful tool in selling; use it to get the most from it.

8. SELLING MUST BE BENEFIT-LED

The concept of benefits, and features, was investigated in Chapter 6 and we shall not return to the details here. Suffice to say that this is a crucial aspect of successful service selling; and something that again can enhance differentiation. Anyone selling a service must be:

» clear what the specific benefits of the service are and able to differentiate them from features (something that needs a little thought and is not quite as obvious as may be thought at first sight);
» able to prioritize and describe benefits appropriately in light of what is known about a particular customer – remember a benefit is a benefit, but not all benefits are relevant to every buyer (someone booking a suite in a top hotel may not be as influenced by a price benefit as someone traveling on a budget, for instance, yet money saved is certainly "a benefit"); and
» able to make benefits predominate in the overall conversation and relate what they do to the overall "weighing up" process that characterizes the way people buy.

Benefits should mostly come first – tell people what they get, then use features to demonstrate how this is possible. This, coupled with the powers of description mentioned above (point 7), makes for a powerful approach at the core of the sales process.

9. SELLING IS A COMPLEX PROCESS AND MUST BE MANAGED

The biggest challenge of selling is perhaps in the management of the whole process. Each individual stage is essentially manageable. But there is a great deal going on. As a sales meeting progresses you have to follow your plan and deal with anything leading you away from it. You need to fine-tune what you are doing to accommodate unanticipated factors along the way (and to do that you have to notice them!). You must listen, concentrate, and judge how you do things as well as what you will do. You must draw with precision from a not inconsiderable body of information about your service, clients, industry, and more, much of which must be held in your head.

Understanding what needs to be done is important here; the best sales people certainly exhibit a real awareness of the details of the process and how it works. So too is confidence, for example you may need to say *I don't know* or pause and say *Let me think about that for a moment* (a much better option than jumping in with an ill-considered answer, though it can be awkward to do it).

Beyond this, what helps? Practice. Which golfer was it who is reputed to have said *It's a funny thing, but the more I practice the more good luck I seem to have*? Selling is a skill we can spend a lifetime learning. It is dynamic and so is the environment in which it operates. Recognize that and you are halfway to dealing with it.

10. SELLING EFFECTIVELY MUST TAKE A LONG-TERM VIEW

A quick meeting followed by a clear agreement. It is nice, but it is certainly not always what happens. As you sell you have to keep the longer-term view in mind. Let me suggest two degrees of time scale that need to be contemplated:

» *The immediate aftermath of a meeting:* this is best illustrated by the occasion when interest seems high, but you cannot get past a kind of *Leave it with me* comment. Here persistence pays off. Keep in touch, arrange to contact the client again, and do so as many times as it takes. It is easy to lose heart as you telephone and are given excuses – *They're in a meeting*. Ask when it finishes, make contact again, and ring the changes in terms of method – ring, write, fax, e-mail. If there really is no prospect, the client will tell you; while there might be possibilities of business, you need to remain fresh in the client's mind, not a competitor. Increased persistence can be an easy, low-cost way of boosting sales.

» *Long-term contact:* after a sale is successfully made (or not, when it may still be worth re-contacting people), make a plan of ongoing contact and avoid losing touch. Seek recommendations, plan a client strategy, analyze the nature especially of large client organizations – it is always easier and less expensive to get more business from those whom you know, who have used your services in the past and found them satisfactory, than to seek out new, but cold, prospects. Nurture what you have; it can pay dividends in the future.

It is difficult, perhaps deceiving, to try to encapsulate a topic such as selling; however, I am confident that these 10 points make sense. In selling intangible services, the details of the matter become even more important, and what can be gained by careful use of those core techniques and of approaches that affect things in key ways is considerable.

Frequently Asked Questions (FAQs)

Q1: How is selling services different from selling products?

A: See Chapter 1, Introduction.

Q2: What does the sales process encompass?

A: See Chapter 2, What Is Service Selling?

Q3: Is sales success affected by how people perceive it?

A: See Chapter 3, The Evolution of Service Selling.

Q4: Selling is a personal skill; is it affected by the IT revolution?

A: See Chapter 4, The E-Dimension.

Q5: Can selling be applied in the same way across the globe?

A: See Chapter 5, The Global Dimension.

Q6: How do the core techniques work?

A: See Chapter 6, The State of the Art.

Q7: How do I maximize my use of sales techniques?

A: See Chapter 7, In Practice.

Q8: Isn't selling just a matter of "clear communications"?

A: There is more to it than that; see Chapter 6, The State of the Art and Chapter 7, In Practice, for details of the complexities of the techniques and approaches to be deployed.

Q9: How do I find out more and keep up to date?

A: See Chapter 9, Resources.

Q10: What needs concentrating on most to ensure success?

A: See Chapter 10, Ten Steps to Making Selling Services Work.

Acknowledgments

I can claim no credit for the origination of the format of the series of which this book is part. So thanks are due to those at Capstone who did so, and for the opportunity they provided for me to play a small part in so significant and novel a publishing project. This title comes as part of phase two of the project and I know, not least from contacts with readers of volumes I contributed to the first series, that its first hundred titles have hit the spot and have been highly successful.

Sales in all its forms – and especially the selling of services – has for long been part of my work portfolio. I began my career on the sales side of a publishing company, progressed (?) to selling training products, courses, and conferences and, having moved into consultancy, to conducting courses on, amongst other things, selling and sales management. My book *Marketing Professional Services* (Kogan Page) acted to extend my service selling involvement further, as did my work with a number of professional institutes in this area (for example, The Institute of Chartered Accountants). I have worked now with a wide range of professional service firms; and continue to do to.

Thanks are due here therefore to many people whom I have met and worked with, or who had attending training programs of one sort or another on different aspects of selling. Their experiences, whether shared willingly or unwittingly, have accelerated my learning and formed the basis of any expertise I may have in what is a fascinating – and vital – part of the overall marketing process.

Patrick Forsyth
Touchstone Training & Consultancy
28 Saltcote Maltings
Maldon
Essex CM9 4QP
United Kingdom

Index

EXPRESSEXEC –
BUSINESS THINKING AT YOUR FINGERTIPS

ExpressExec is a 12-module resource with 10 titles in each module. Combined they form a complete resource of current business practice. Each title enables the reader to quickly understand the key concepts and models driving management thinking today.

Available from:
www.expressexec.com

Customer Service Department
John Wiley & Sons Ltd
Southern Cross Trading Estate
1 Oldlands Way, Bognor Regis
West Sussex, PO22 9SA
Tel: +44(0)1243 843 294
Fax: +44(0)1243 843 303
Email: cs-books@wiley.co.uk

Printed and bound by CPI Group (UK) Ltd, Croydon, CR0 4YY

14/04/2025

14656898-0001